Cooking With Care

Please join the volunteers, staff and families of
HospiceCare of the Piedmont, Inc.
as they share their family recipes.

The purpose of HospiceCare of the Piedmont, Inc. is to provide physical, spiritual and psychosocial care and education related to end-of-life care based on the Hospice Philosophy for the terminally ill, their families and the communities served.

Copies of *Cooking With Care* may be obtained by sending $19.95 plus $5.00 shipping and handling to the following address. South Carolina residents should add $1.20 sales tax. For your convenience, order forms are located in the back of the cookbook.

HospiceCare of the Piedmont, Inc.
408 West Alexander Avenue
Greenwood, South Carolina 29646
(864) 227-9393 Office
(864) 227-9377 Fax

Printed in the USA by
WIMMER
The Wimmer Companies
Memphis
1-800-548-2537

Table of Contents

Cookbook Development

Editor
Cheryl Barnhart

Section Chairs
Ruby Adams
Angie Barnhart
Margie Bratcher
Kanda Brunson
Fran Garland
Ruth Goldman
Delsie Horne
Peggy Ticehurst

Section Editors
Ruby Clark
Carolyn Strom
Sandy Walter

Art Work
Camilla Marchi

Heartfelt Appreciation To
Hsueh-an White of Frames Unlimited
who did the matting for the art work
in memory of White family members.

Restaurant Contributors

Belmont Inn
Court Square
Abbeville, South Carolina

Coffee & Dessert Co.
217 Waller Avenue - Uptown Exchange
Greenwood, South Carolina

The Gatewood Club
114 Club Drive
Greenwood, South Carolina

Pascal's Café & Grill
307 West Cambridge Avenue
Greenwood, South Carolina

Regan's Restaurant on Main
328 Main Street
Greenwood, South Carolina

Somebody's House
5206 Emerson Street
Hodges, South Carolina

Country Kitchen
Saluda, South Carolina

All About Us...

HospiceCare of the Piedmont, Inc. was established in 1981 as part of a massive spread of compassion and caring throughout our country which is now known as the "Hospice Movement". A concept of caring for the terminally ill, which was pioneered in London, had found its way to the United States and to our area of rural, upstate South Carolina.

As word of this "special kind of caring" spread, some interested individuals within the Greenwood medical community were paying attention. It was a philosophy of care which addressed not only patient's needs but their families' needs as well.

HospiceCare exists to provide the special kind of care designed to provide sensitivity and support for patients and families facing the physical and emotional challenge of a life-limiting illness. This care is available to patients when efforts toward cure are no longer indicated. Under the direction of the primary physician, our goal is to enhance the patient's quality of life by managing symptoms, controlling pain, and helping create the most comfortable environment possible.

HospiceCare of the Piedmont has provided hospice care for twenty years. Because of the generosity of special people in the community, services are provided regardless of a pay source. Since 1981, over 3,000 patients have benefited from hospice services. Our program is owned and supported by the communities served. The impact of hospice on the lives of patients and families has been enormous. The goals of hospice continues to be directed toward the enhancement of services as well as assuring that compassionate, competent hospice care is available and accessible to those in need.

"You matter because you are you. You matter to the last moment of your life, and we will do all we can, not only to help you die peacefully, but also to live until you die."

Dame Cicely Saunders,
Founder of the Modern Hospice Movement

In Memory of Mrs. Jessie Julien

Many personalities have added beautiful color, texture and freshness to the garden of HospiceCare and to its activities. Each individual's contribution is unique and each is additive to the making of the whole - interweaving into the beautiful fabric of Hospice. On May 18, 1999, one of the loveliest of all roses in our garden of life was taken from us to be added to the centerpiece of God's banquet table. Mrs. Jessie Julien will always be remembered as one of the strongest supporters of our Hospice. Her dedication, commitment and example of graceful living and her sharing of herself and her resources shall forever remain exemplary.

Mrs. Julien wished to be personally involved and on many occasions baked one of her delicious pound cakes or made her soothing boiled custard to be delivered to the patient by one of our volunteers. This always made for a cheerful visit, brought forth a smile, adding a spark of happiness to that special patient on that special day.

Each of us associated with Hospice benefited by her keen intellect, infectious sense of humor and colorful personality. She shared humbly with us her collection of almost 104 years of wisdom and insight into living. Her sense of fairness and her appreciation of each given day allowed her to demonstrate so remarkably the art of living to the fullest and aging gracefully. To have associated with this extraordinary personality and to be able to call her friend and confidante is a treasure beyond all measure.

We all realize that our lives were touched by a very special angel and were challenged to be the very best that we could be for all the patients we care for. She demonstrated contentment and gratefulness and was able to find happiness in whatever state she found herself. She taught us that truly it is our dedication to cause and our service to others that bring us to happiness and completeness.

So we dedicate this book to Mrs. Julien as a token expression of our love for her. In the sorrow of her absence, we are sustained by our beautiful memories of this truly remarkable lady and friend.

K. Jack Parham, M.D.
Medical Director

Mrs. Julien's Famous Pound Cake

Made for Hospice patients for many years.

2   **sticks butter**
1   **stick margarine**
3   **cups white sugar**
5   **eggs**
3   **cups flour**
1   **cup milk**
¾   **teaspoon vanilla**
¾   **teaspoon lemon extract**

- Preheat oven to 350°.
- Grease and flour a 10 inch tube or Bundt pan. (May cover bottom with wax paper.) Set aside.
- In a large mixing bowl, cream together butter, margarine and sugar; mix thoroughly.
- Add eggs one at a time, beating well after each addition.
- Add about ⅓ of the flour and milk. Beat until batter is as smooth as can be. Keep adding the flour and milk alternately and beating well after each addition.
- Add vanilla and lemon extracts.
- Pour batter into prepared pan. Cover pan with aluminum foil the first 30 minutes of baking. Bake at 350° for 1 hour or more. Test with straw. If straw comes out clean, the cake is done. Remove from oven and put in brown grocery bag for 10 minutes.

Serves 12 to 14

The lady that shared this recipe was almost 104 years old when she died. In her generation, broom straws were commonly used to test cakes for doneness.

Camilla Marchi

Camilla Marchi, more commonly known as Cam, is a registered nurse who retired from HospiceCare of the Piedmont in January, 2000, after 10 years of service as a staff nurse. She lives in the small village of Abbeville, South Carolina. Cam is a native of Georgia, married with three children and five grandchildren. She and husband John (also a hospice volunteer) travel a great deal since her retirement.

She states that she has always held a love for art, drawing and painting. She has studied with a number of noted artists. Portraiture has now become her first love, although she has received a number of private commissions for both portraits and landscapes. Presently, a group of paintings -INDIAN WOMEN- will be on exhibit at the Catawba Cultural Preservation Museum in Rock Hill, South Carolina. Cam says that "her goal for any painting would be that it revives a loving or cherished memory for the viewer".

Cookbook Sponsors

Heart of Hospice

Knight Industries, Inc.

Angel

Capsugel-Division of Pfizer

Dove

Atheneum Study Club
Greenwood Packing Plant
George W. Park Seed Co., Inc.
Wal-Mart

Star

Bill Boyd Realty, Inc.
Davis & Floyd, Inc.
Family of Kathleen Frihart
Greenwood Fabricating & Plating, Inc.
Flexible Technologies
Mountain Bank
Dawn Sease, Realtor
SPC, Inc.
Stoney Point Golf Community
Our Lady of Lourdes Catholic Church
Velux-Greenwood, Inc.

Appetizers and Beverages

Appetizers

Beverages

Shrimp and Lobster Salsa

2   lobster tails
¼   pound shrimp
2   tablespoons seafood boil
1   large green bell pepper, chopped
1   large yellow pepper, chopped
1   large red pepper, chopped
3   large green peppers (use selective peppers depending on how
        hot you prefer)
5   Roma tomatoes, chopped
3   large garden tomatoes, chopped
1   red onion, chopped
½   tablespoon black pepper
½   tablespoon cayenne pepper
1   lime
1   small bunch cilantro, chopped

- Boil lobster tails and shrimp (peeled or unpeeled) in water and seafood boil until done. Drain, cool, peel or take out of shell; chop to size of peppers.

- Combine peppers, tomatoes, onion, black pepper, cayenne pepper, juice from lime (discard lime) and cilantro.

- Add seafood to vegetable mixture; refrigerate at least 4 hours.

- Serve with assorted tortilla chips.

Serves 15 to 30

This wonderful salsa recipe was shared with us by native Greenwoodian, Regan Marshall. In 1996, he returned from Charleston to make his dream of owning a restaurant come true. In 1997, his father became a special partner and works side by side with Regan. Located in uptown Greenwood, Regan's offers a full menu, including everything from delicious appetizers to delectable desserts.

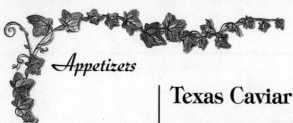

Texas Caviar

2   (14 ounce) cans black-eyed peas, rinsed and drained
1   (15 ounce) can white hominy, drained
6   ounces Italian saladdressing
1   medium green pepper, diced
4   green onions, chopped
2   garlic cloves, minced
1   small onion, chopped
2   jalapeño peppers, seeded and diced
½   cup fresh parsley, chopped
2   tablespoons lime juice (optional)
3-4 medium tomatoes, chopped
1   (8 ounce) jar salsa or picante sauce
     Tortilla chips

- In large bowl, combine peas, hominy, Italian dressing, green pepper, onions, garlic, jalapeño peppers and parsley. If desired, add lime juice at this point. Refrigerate overnight.
- About 2 hours before serving, add tomatoes and salsa.
- Serve with tortilla chips.

7 cups

If a Mexican theme is desired, serve tortilla chips around a sombrero with 'caviar' in bowl in the center of the hat.

Creamy Sausage Dip

This dish is deceptively simple, but the recipe is always requested.

1   **pound pork sausage**
1   **(8 ounce) package cream cheese, softened**
1   **(10 ounce) can tomatoes with green chiles**

- In skillet, brown sausage until crumbly and no longer pink. Drain on paper towels.
- Stir in cream cheese and tomatoes.
- Spread mixture in small casserole dish and bake in preheated 325° oven until hot and bubbly.

Serves 10

Cheesy Vidalia Onion Dip

1   **large sweet onion, finely chopped**
1   **cup mayonnaise**
1   **cup Parmesan cheese, grated**
     Bagel chips or crackers

- Combine onion, mayonnaise and cheese.
- Bake uncovered at 350° for 30 minutes.
- Serve with bagel chips, tortilla chips, or crackers.

2 cups

A Gift of Love

"All of our caregivers made my family member's last days very happy. He always looked forward to their coming. They gave him hope and love. All of them made my part much easier and I cannot thank all of you enough. Hospice is a wonderful gift to the sick and their families. Words cannot express just how much I thank all of you for your concern for my family and me. You lift my spirits every time you come. May God shed many, many blessings upon each of you and your families. Love in Christ and bless you."

Artichoke and Rye Crisps

2   **(14 ounce) cans artichoke hearts, well drained**
2   **(6 ounce) jars marinated artichoke hearts, well drained**
4   **tablespoons mayonnaise**
2   **teaspoons Worcestershire sauce**
¼   **teaspoon garlic powder**
1   **teaspoon Cavender's Greek seasoning**
    Salt to taste
1½ **cups dry bread crumbs**
1-2 **drops Tabasco sauce**
2   **tablespoons lemon juice**
4   **tablespoons butter, melted**
1   **(5 ounce) package fresh Romano cheese, finely shredded, divided**
    Party rye bread, cut in halves (or fourths)

- Mix artichokes, mayonnaise, Worcestershire sauce, garlic powder, Greek seasoning, salt, bread crumbs, Tabasco, lemon juice, and butter in food processor or blender.
- Stir in 3 tablespoons of the cheese.
- Spread about 1 teaspoon of the mixture on the cut bread.
- Sprinkle cheese on top or place cheese in a saucer and dip the spread side of the bread into the cheese.
- Bake on a cookie sheet at 350° for 10 minutes, or until rye bread is lightly browned and cheese melted.

Serves 20 to 25

Freezes well. Thaw before using.

Intimidated by an Artichoke?

To prepare artichokes first cut off the stem end and slice about ½ inch from the top of each artichoke. Trim away about ¼ of each outer leaf, using kitchen shears. Rub top of artichoke and edges of leaves with lemon juice to prevent discoloration. Place in a large Dutch oven; add water to depth of 1 inch. Add salt to water; bring to a full boil. Cover and reduce heat; simmer 25 minutes or until almost tender. Many people just don't know how to go about eating this delectable vegetable. Pluck the cooked leaves, one at a time, dipping the base of the leaf into clarified butter or sauce of your choice. Turn the leaf meaty side down, and draw the leaf between the teeth, scraping off the meaty portion. When you are finished with the leaves, there will remain a core of little leaves and a

Artichoke Squares

2   **(6 ounce) jars marinated artichoke hearts**
1   **medium onion, chopped**
2   **garlic cloves, minced**
4   **eggs, beaten**
½   **cup bread crumbs**
½   **teaspoon Tabasco sauce**
½   **teaspoon oregano**
½   **teaspoon salt**
½   **teaspoon pepper**
2   **cups shredded Cheddar cheese**

- Drain artichokes, reserving the liquid of 1 jar.
- Heat reserved liquid in a medium skillet. Add the onion and garlic. Sauté until tender.
- Chop the artichokes. Combine artichokes, eggs, bread crumbs, Tabasco sauce, oregano, salt, pepper, cheese and onion mixture in a medium bowl and mix well.
- Spread mixture in a 9 x 13 inch baking dish.
- Bake at 325° for 30 minutes.
- Cut into squares. Serve warm.

30 squares

fuzzy "choke". Cut off the center core of leaves, and slice off the choke with a knife and fork. The remaining "heart" is considered the prize portion of the vegetable; cut it into bite-size pieces and dip into the sauce.

Jalapeño Pepper Appetizers

These are habit-forming!

20 medium jalapeño peppers, fresh
1   (8 ounce) package cream cheese
10 bacon strips, halved

• Cut peppers in half lengthwise; remove seeds, stems and center membrane. Make sure you wear rubber gloves for this process!
• Stuff each half with cream cheese.
• Wrap with bacon and secure with toothpick.
• Place on broiler rack that has been coated with nonstick cooking spray.
• Bake at 350° for 20 to 25 minutes or until bacon is crisp. Remove toothpicks.

40 appetizers

BLT Spread

The bacon filling also makes a chunky dressing for a salad.

1   cup mayonnaise
1   (8 ounce) carton sour cream
1   pound bacon, fried and crumbled
2-3 large tomatoes, peeled, seeded and chopped
    Assorted crackers

• Combine mayonnaise and sour cream in a medium bowl, stirring well with a whisk.
• Stir in bacon and tomatoes.
• Keep chilled until serving time. Serve with crackers.

3 to 4 cups

This may also be used as a dip served in Belgian endive leaves.

Taco Cheesecake

1 **cup crushed tortilla chips**
1 **tablespoon butter or margarine, melted**
1 **pound ground round**
1 **(1¾ ounce) envelope taco seasoning mix, divided**
2 **tablespoons water**
2 **(8 ounce) packages cream cheese, softened**
2 **large eggs**
2 **cups Cheddar cheese**
1 **(8 ounce) carton sour cream**
2 **tablespoons all-purpose flour**
  Shredded lettuce
  Tomato, chopped
  Green bell pepper, diced

- Preheat oven to 325°
- Stir together tortilla chips and butter. Press into bottom of a 9-inch spring form pan.
- Bake for 10 minutes. Cool on wire rack.
- Brown beef in large skillet over medium heat, stirring until crumbly and no longer pink. Drain and pat dry.
- Return beef to skillet. Reserving 1 teaspoon taco seasoning, stir remaining taco seasoning and 2 tablespoons water into beef. Cook over medium heat, stirring occasionally, 5 minutes or until liquid evaporates.
- Beat cream cheese at medium speed with an electric mixer until fluffy; add eggs and reserved 1 teaspoon taco seasoning mix, beating until blended. Add Cheddar cheese and beat until blended.
- Spread cream cheese mixture evenly over crust and 1 inch up sides of pan.
- Spoon in beef mixture.
- Spread cream cheese mixture from around sides of pan over beef mixture, forming a 1-inch border.
- Combine sour cream and flour and spread over cheesecake.
- Bake for 25 minutes. Cool in pan on wire rack for 10 minutes.
- Run knife around edges; release sides.
- Serve warm with toppings.

Serves 12

Salmon Pâté

Easy, elegant and delicious

8   ounces fresh salmon filet, cooked or 8 ounces canned red
      salmon, drained, skinned and boned
½   cup cottage cheese
1   teaspoon lemon juice
¼   teaspoon nutmeg (optional)
¼   teaspoon Tabasco sauce
      Salt and pepper to taste
2   tablespoons sour cream
      Pinch of paprika
      Sprigs of dill

* In food processor or bowl, combine the salmon and cottage cheese.
* Add lemon juice, nutmeg, Tabasco sauce, salt, sour cream, and paprika.
* Mix until thoroughly blended.
* Pour into a serving dish and chill.
* To serve, decorate with small sprigs of dill.

Serves 8 to 10

When using canned fish, the flavor seems to improve if the can is chilled before opening.

Mushroom Mousse Neufchâtel

This is a mellow appetizer - almost comfort food

1	tablespoon butter
⅓	cup shallots, chopped
8	ounces mushrooms, chopped
2	cloves garlic, minced
¼	teaspoon salt
¼	teaspoon pepper
4	ounces Neufchâtel cheese
	Touch of lemon juice (optional)

- In Skillet, melt butter, add shallots and sauté for 1 minute.
- Add mushrooms, garlic, salt and pepper.
- Sauté for about 5 minutes until mushrooms release their juices.
- Raise heat and cook until mixture is almost dry. Remove from heat and cool.
- In a food processor, blend mushroom mixture with cheese and lemon juice until smooth.
- Adjust seasoning and chill.
- Good served with Melba toast rounds.

Serves 8 to 10

*Dear
Hospice Staff,*

"I cannot call names for I might forget someone and I could never do that because *everyone of you are wonderful*. You have been a blessing to all of us and we love you. Thank you again and again. God loves you and so do we."

Stuffed Pea Pods

Pea pods lend themselves beautifully to all sorts of other stuffings as well; two or three different stuffings on a tray make for a very decorative and appealing appetizer.

½ **pound fresh Chinese pea pods**
Crabmeat filling (recipe follows)
Bleu Cheese filling (recipe follows)

• Wash pea pods, and blanch for 1 to 2 minutes. Remove tough stems and slit lengthwise at the top.
• Fill with crabmeat filling or bleu cheese filling.

Crabmeat Filling
¼ **cup mayonnaise**
½ **cup crabmeat, fresh or canned**
1 **scallion, chopped**
2 **tablespoons parsley, chopped**

• Combine mayonnaise, crabmeat, scallion and parsley. Mix thoroughly and refrigerate until ready for filling pea pods.

Bleu Cheese Filling
¼ **cup bleu cheese, crumbled**
3 **ounces cream cheese**
2 **tablespoons milk**

• Combine bleu cheese, cream cheese and milk. Mix thoroughly and refrigerate until ready for filling pea pods.

About 40 pods

Smoked Salmon Parcels
with Lemon Cheese and Capers

This recipe is also delicious prepared with very thinly sliced roast beef and substituting horseradish for the lemon zest and juice.

30 **slices smoked salmon**
12 **ounces cream cheese**
   Zest from 2 lemons
   Juice from 1 lemon
   Salt to taste
   Pepper, generous amount
2 **tablespoons capers, drained**
1 **bunch fresh dill**
   Cucumber slices

- Cut salmon slices in halves or thirds, depending on size.
- In a food processor or a bowl, blend cream cheese, zest, juice (reserve second lemon for more juice if needed to soften cheese), salt, pepper and capers.
- Roll a bit of the cheese mixture in the salmon slices.
- Secure with a toothpick.
- Garnish with cucumber slices and small sprigs of dill.

Serves 10 to 12

"My mother's nurses were so sweet and she loved them very much".

Spinach Roulade with Smoked Salmon & Red Pepper Sauce

This dish is beautiful. Food that looks and tastes this good makes a memorable party table.

2	pounds fresh spinach or 16 ounces frozen
1	egg yolk
1	teaspoon garlic powder
	Pinch nutmeg
	Salt and pepper to taste
4	egg whites
1	cup low fat cottage cheese
4	ounces light cream cheese
2	teaspoons fresh dill or ½ teaspoon dried
4	ounces smoked salmon, chopped

- Preheat oven to 375°.
- Line jelly roll pan with parchment paper, and spray lightly with cooking spray.
- If using fresh spinach, remove stalks from leaves and rinse; cook 2 to 3 minutes until limp, and chop. Cook frozen spinach according to package directions, then drain and chop.
- Beat egg yolk into spinach; add garlic powder, nutmeg, salt and pepper. Set aside.
- Whisk egg whites until stiff, but not dry.
- Fold egg whites into spinach mixture, pour mixture into pan; bake 10 minutes.
- In a food processor, mix cottage cheese, cream cheese and dill; blend until smooth.
- In small bowl, fold smoked salmon into cheese mixture until blended.
- When roulade is cooked, turn it out onto a damp dish towel and remove parchment paper. Trim the edge and spread filling over roulade.
- Roll up roulade using the aid of the towel. Chill or serve slightly warm with Red Pepper Sauce.

Serves 8 to 10

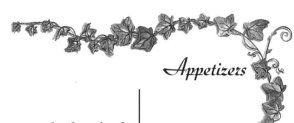

Red Pepper Sauce

*For the bouquet garni, try fresh thyme, rosemary and a bay leaf
- tie it together with cooking twine. Or choose your favorite
herbs and spices.*

1   **medium red bell pepper, quartered, pith and seeds removed**
1   **small onion, chopped**
1   **teaspoon olive oil**
1   **peeled and seeded tomato**
1   **clove garlic, minced**
     Bouquet garni
6   **tablespoons water**

* Heat broiler, and singe pepper on the skin side until black all
  over.* Remove skin and cut flesh into strips.
* Sauté onion in oil until soft. Add tomato, red pepper, garlic and
  bouquet garni.
* Add 6 tablespoons water, bring to boil, cover and simmer
  20 minutes.
* Remove bouquet garni. Pour mixture into blender and process
  until smooth. Pass through a sieve and chill.

** Place roasted bell perrers in a Zip-loc bag for approximately
10 minutes; skins will then slide off easily.*

At the turn of the twentieth century, there were many "road companies" producing shows in New York City. Once the production was assembled, the show traveled throughout the country. One of the more popular tours went from New York to Richmond to Atlanta. For a number of years, Abbeville was an overnight stop for the entire touring company. Several members of the community decided that if this area had a facility, since the traveling companies were coming through here anyway, Abbeville should sponsor some of these productions.

King Crab Appetizers

These are a family favorite at holiday get-togethers.

2   (12 ounce) packages refrigerated biscuit dough
1   (8 ounce) package cream cheese, softened
1   (6 ounce) can crabmeat, drained
2   tablespoons mayonnaise
2   tablespoons grated Parmesan cheese
½   cup shredded Cheddar cheese
2   tablespoons finely chopped green onion
1   teaspoon Worcestershire sauce
    Pinch paprika

- Preheat oven to 375°.
- Lightly grease 12 tartlet pans.
- Divide each biscuit in half and press into the prepared muffin tin. Set aside.
- In a large bowl, combine cream cheese, crab, mayonnaise, Parmesan cheese, Cheddar cheese, green onions and Worcestershire sauce. Spoon 1 teaspoon mixture into tarts and garnish with paprika.
- Bake 15 to 20 minutes, or until light brown.

Serves 12

These freeze wonderfully. Just reheat before serving.

Crab Delights

Serve these as appetizers or a light lunch. May be made ahead and frozen; bake when ready to use.

1	**(6 ounce) can crabmeat, drained**
5	**ounces sharp processed cheese spread**
¼	**cup butter, softened**
2	**tablespoons mayonnaise**
1	**pinch garlic salt**
2	**tablespoons chopped fresh parsley**
6	**English muffins, split in half**

- Preheat oven to 400°.
- In medium size mixing bowl, combine crabmeat, cheese spread, butter, mayonnaise, garlic salt and parsley. Mix well.
- Spread mixture on English muffins. Cut muffins into triangles and place on cookie sheet.
- Bake 15 minutes.
- Place under broiler for last minute or two of baking time to brown tops.

48 triangles

On October 1, 1908, what was then the Abbeville District, dedicated a new Court House and City Hall. The grand old theater now known as the Abbeville Opera House was a part of that splendid pair of buildings. Some months later, the great stage was officially used for its intended purpose. The show was called "The Clansman" and it was a gala occasion that set the entire area buzzing with excitement.

Broiled Onion Toasts

Perfect as an appetizer or served on the side of a hearty dinner salad.

1	**cup Parmesan cheese, grated**
1	**medium onion, finely chopped**
1	**cup mayonnaise**
	Dash white pepper
1	**loaf cocktail bread**

- Mix cheese, onion, mayonnaise and pepper together.
- Spread mixture on little cocktail bread slices.
- Broil open faced sandwiches in the broiler until browned. Serve warm.

Serves 18

Chicken Triangles

1	pound boneless, skinless chicken breast, fat removed
½	teaspoon olive oil
2	tablespoons lemon juice
2	cloves garlic, minced
1	tablespoon fresh parsley, minced
½	tablespoon fresh tarragon leaf, chopped
½	tablespoon fresh basil, chopped
	Salt to taste
10	sheets phyllo pastry
3	tablespoons melted butter or corn oil

- Preheat oven to 400°.
- Mince chicken and combine in a bowl with olive oil, lemon juice, garlic, parsley, tarragon, basil and salt. Chill about 1 hour.
- On a flat surface, lay out one sheet of phyllo and brush with the butter or oil; repeat with a second sheet, on top of the first one.
- Cut phyllo in 5 equal strips across; lay about 1 tablespoon of the chicken mixture on the end of each strip.
- Fold diagonally, back and forth on each strip, to make a triangle.
- Repeat this with the other 8 sheets.
- Place on a baking sheet lined with parchment paper. Bake about 15 minutes or until golden brown.

Serves 25

Parmesan Cheese Straws

This is one of those handy recipes that makes a fast yet elegant party pleaser. Serve alongside a cheese and olive assortment for an appetizer plate.

6   **sheets phyllo dough**
4   **tablespoons unsalted butter, melted**
1   **cup freshly grated good-quality Parmesan cheese**

- Preheat oven to 350°.
- Cut phyllo dough in half widthwise. Brush each half lightly with butter, using a pastry brush.
- Sprinkle each with 2 teaspoons cheese. Roll up tightly like a cigar, so that it is 11 inches long and ½ inch wide.
- Brush the tops with more melted butter and sprinkle evenly with 1½ to 2 teaspoons cheese.
- Place on ungreased baking sheet. Bake for 10 to 15 minutes, until golden brown and crisp. Serve at room temperature.

Serves 12

Mexican Wontons

These are crispy, cheese-filled appetizers. Serve with salsa.

1   **pound pepper-jack cheese, finely shredded**
1   **(14 ounce) package wonton wrappers**
1   **cup vegetable oil**

- Place 1 to 2 teaspoons of cheese into the center of each wonton skin. Fold the top and bottom corners in toward each other and roll it up like a little egg roll. You will have to seal the wonton with a little water where the ends meet.
- Heat oil in a deep pot to 365°. Fry the wontons two or three at a time. Drain on paper towels. Serve while hot.

Serves 10 to 15

These can be prepared ahead of time and reheated in the oven until they sizzle before serving.

"Our mother looked forward to your visits, loved each of you and valued your friendship."

Mini Chicken Turnovers

These turnovers make great appetizers and they're worth the extra effort because they're simply delicious.

3   tablespoons chopped onion
3   tablespoons butter
1¾ cups shredded, cooked chicken
3   tablespoons chicken broth
¼   teaspoon garlic salt
¼   teaspoon poultry seasoning
¼   teaspoon ground black pepper
1   (3 ounce) package cream cheese, diced
1½ cups all-purpose flour
½   teaspoon salt
½   teaspoon paprika
1   cup butter, chilled
5   tablespoons cold water

- Preheat oven to 375°.
- In large skillet, sauté the onion in the butter until tender. Stir in the chicken, broth, garlic salt, poultry seasoning, pepper and cream cheese. Remove from heat and set aside.
- In a large mixing bowl, mix together flour, salt and paprika; cut in butter until mixture resembles coarse crumbs. Gradually add water, tossing with a fork until a ball forms.
- On a floured surface, roll out the pastry to ¹⁄₁₆ inch thick. Cut with a 2½ inch round cookie or biscuit cutter. Re-roll scraps and cut more circles until the pastry is used up.
- Mound a heaping teaspoon of filling on half of each circle.
- Moisten edges with water and fold pastry over filling to make a half moon shape. Press edges with a fork to seal. Prick tops with fork for steam vents.
- Place turnovers on a baking sheet and bake 15 to 20 minutes or until golden brown.

2½ dozen

For do-ahead appetizers, these can be baked, frozen and reheated at 375° for 5 to 7 minutes.

Crescent Roll Deli Pie

Small slices can be served as an appetizer, or serve large slices with a salad for a meal.

2 **(8 ounce) packages refrigerated crescent rolls**
¼ **pound thinly sliced ham**
¼ **pound thinly sliced hard salami**
¼ **pound thinly sliced pepperoni**
¼ **pound thinly sliced provolone cheese**
1 **egg, beaten**

- Preheat oven to 350°.
- Spread out 1 can of crescent rolls in bottom of 9 x 13 inch casserole dish.
- Layer meat and cheese in any order and combination, according to your taste. Cover with the second can of crescent rolls over the top and pinch the edges so they close as if making a pie.
- Brush the egg on top layer of rolls. Using a fork, prick holes in the top layer to vent.
- Bake about 15 minutes, or until golden brown.
- Cut cooked "deli pie" into squares, triangles, or other serving shape desired. Can be served hot or cold.

Serves 18 to 20 appetizers

Spinach and Artichokes in Puff Pastry

1   (10 ounce) package frozen chopped spinach, thawed
1   (14 ounce) can artichoke hearts, drained and chopped
½   cup mayonnaise
½   cup grated Parmesan cheese
1   teaspoon onion powder
1   teaspoon garlic powder
½   teaspoon white pepper
1   (17.3 ounce) package frozen puff pastry

- Preheat oven to 400°.
- Drain spinach well, pressing between layers of paper towels.
- Stir together spinach, artichoke hearts, mayonnaise, cheese, onion powder, garlic powder and pepper.
- Thaw puff pastry at room temperature 30 minutes. Unfold pastry, and place on a lightly floured surface or heavy-duty plastic wrap. Spread one-fourth spinach mixture evenly over pastry sheet, leaving a ½ inch border.
- Roll up pastry jelly roll fashion, pressing to seal seam; wrap in heavy-duty plastic wrap. Repeat procedure with remaining pastry and spinach mixture.
- Freeze 30 minutes; cut into ½ inch-thick slices. (Rolls may be frozen up to 3 months.)
- Bake for 20 minutes or until golden brown.

4 dozen

Taco Ring

1   **pound lean ground beef, cooked and drained**
1   **package taco seasoning mix**
1   **cup shredded sharp Cheddar cheese**
2   **tablespoons water**
2   **(8 ounce) packages refrigerated crescent rolls**
½   **head iceberg lettuce, shredded**
1   **medium tomato, chopped**
1   **small onion, chopped**
1   **(4 ounce) can black olives, sliced**
1   **cup salsa**
1   **medium bell pepper, cored**
     Sour cream

- Preheat oven to 350°.
- Combine meat, seasoning mix, cheese and water together.
- Arrange the crescent triangles in a circle on a round baking stone or pizza pan with the bases overlapping each other in the center with the points going toward the outside. There should be a 5 inch diameter in the center.
- Spoon the meat mixture on each triangle. Fold the points of each triangle over the top of the meat mixture and press into the bottom of the base. The filling will not be completely covered.
- Bake for 20 to 25 minutes or until golden brown.
- Fill center of ring with lettuce. Top with the chopped tomatoes, onions and olives.
- Pour the salsa into pepper. Top with sour cream.

Serves 8 to 10

The Burt-Stark House

This house was the site of the most dramatic and important event in the history of Abbeville when in May, 1865, Confederate President Jefferson Davis held his last war council there. The house was built by David Lesley in 1841. His wife, Louise, saw a house in the Hudson Valley which they liked. According to family tradition, they sent their slave carpenter, Cubic, on horseback to examine the house, and he built their new house accordingly. Now a National Landmark, the Burt-Stark Mansion (c. 1841), was built in the Greek Revival style.

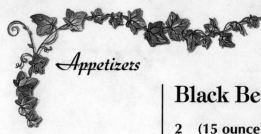

Black Bean Salsa

2	(15 ounce) cans black beans, rinsed and drained
1	(17 ounce) can whole kernel corn, drained
2	large tomatoes, seeded and chopped
1	large avocado, peeled and chopped
⅛	cup chopped, fresh cilantro
3-4	tablespoons lime juice
2	tablespoons olive oil
1	tablespoon red wine vinegar
1	teaspoon salt
½	teaspoon pepper
	Tortilla chips

- Combine beans, corn, tomatoes, avocado, cilantro, lime juice, oil, vinegar, salt and pepper in a large bowl and stir well. Cover and chill.
- Garnish with avocado slices and fresh cilantro. Serve with tortilla chips.

"Our nurse was so great. She made sure our family member was comfortable, she went way beyond and touched us with her caring and love of people."

Sun-Dried Tomato-Basil Spread

1½ ounces sun-dried tomatoes
1 cup olive oil
1 large clove garlic
2 parsley sprigs
5 fresh basil leaves or 1 teaspoon dried leaf basil
¼ teaspoon cayenne pepper
½ teaspoon salt
Pinch sugar
1 green onion, coarsely chopped
2 (4 ounce) goat cheese rounds
Spicy Toast Rounds

- Place the tomatoes in boiling water and then reduce the heat to low until soft (8 to 10 minutes).

- Place the tomatoes, oil, garlic, parsley, basil, pepper, salt, sugar and green onion in an airtight container. Shake to blend ingredients; refrigerate overnight or up to 2 days to blend the flavors.

- To serve, process the contents of the container in a food processor with a steel blade until almost smooth, leaving some texture.

- Place goat cheese on 1 or 2 serving dishes and pour tomato spread over the cheese. Use a small knife to spread on toast rounds or crackers.

Serves 8 to 10

An Abbevillian, Anne Marie Cromer Seigler, organized the first Girls' Tomato Club in the country, the forerunner of today's 4-H Clubs.

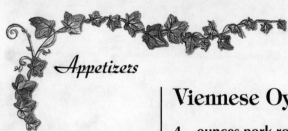

Viennese Oysters

4   ounces pork roll*, cut finely
4   slices lean bacon, cut finely
4   ounces butter
½   cup minced green onion
1-2 cloves garlic, minced
2   cups unseasoned bread crumbs
1½ cups Parmesan cheese, grated
24 ounces fresh oysters, drained and rinsed
1½ cups Chablis
⅓   cup shredded Cheddar cheese
    Thinly sliced toast triangles and assorted crackers.

- Preheat oven to 350°.
- In microwave-safe dish, crisp bacon and pork roll for 3 to 5 minutes.
- In medium skillet, sauté onion and garlic in butter.
- Add bread crumbs, stirring until medium brown.
- Remove from heat and stir in Parmesan cheese.
- Place oysters in an 11 x 7 inch baking dish. Sprinkle bacon/pork roll mixture over oysters.
- Pour Chablis over the oysters.
- Top with ½ of the bread crumb mixture. Sprinkle Cheddar on top and cover with remaining bread crumb mixture.
- Bake 30 minutes.

Serves 12 to 18

* We tested using Taylor's brand pork roll.

Citrus Iced Tea

Beat the heat with this refreshing beverage.

3   cups water
2   cloves
1   family-size tea bag
1½ cups pineapple juice
½   cup orange juice
2-4 tablespoons fresh lemon juice
⅔   cup sugar
Orange slices, lime slices (optional)

- Bring water and cloves to a boil over medium heat.
- Reduce heat and simmer about 10 minutes.
- Remove from heat; add tea bag and steep 10 minutes.
- Discard tea bag and cloves.
- Add pineapple juice, orange juice, lemon juice and sugar, stirring to dissolve sugar.
- Chill and serve over crushed ice. May garnish with orange/lime slices.

Try mixing 1 quart sweetened iced tea with 1 quart cranmango juice for a very refreshing summer drink. Pour into a tall iced glass and serve with a thin slice of lime.

5 cups

Fresh Lemonade

1½ cups sugar
½   cup boiling water
1½ cups fresh lemon juice (6 to 8 large lemons)
5   cups cold water

- Stir sugar and boiling water until sugar is dissolved.
- Stir in lemon juice and cold water.

8 cups

May substitute fresh lime juice for lemon juice.

Watermelon Punch

This is a refreshing variation of a fresh fruit "ade"

2½ **cups water**
⅔ **cup fresh lemon juice (3 large lemons)**
⅔ **cup sugar**
2 **cups fresh orange juice (about 7 oranges)**
1 **small watermelon, peeled, cubed and seeded**

- Bring water, lemon juice and sugar to a boil. Cool completely.
- Stir in orange juice.
- Process watermelon in blender until smooth and pour through strainer, reserving 3 cups juice. Discard pulp.
- Stir together watermelon juice and sugar mixture.
- Chill thoroughly. Served over crushed ice.

8 cups

Spiced Peach Delight

1 **cup frozen peach slices, thawed**
½ **cup lemon flavored sparkling mineral water**
¼ **teaspoon ground ginger**
1 **(8 ounce) container lemon yogurt, low-fat**
Ground nutmeg or cinnamon

- Combine peaches, mineral water and ginger in container of an electric blender or processor. Pour mixture into a small pitcher; gently stir in yogurt.
- Sprinkle with nutmeg or cinnamon if desired. Serve chilled

2 cups

Orange Street Punch

8	**cups water**
2	**cups sugar**
5	**large bananas, pureed**
1	**(46 ounce) can pineapple juice**
2	**(12 ounce) cans frozen orange juice**
72	**ounces water**
½	**cup lemon juice**
2	**quarts ginger ale**
	Fresh fruit for garnishing

- Combine water and 2 cups sugar in large pot. Boil for 10 minutes, cool.
- Add bananas, pineapple juice, orange juice, 72 ounces water and lemon juice to the sugar syrup.
- Mix thoroughly; freeze six hours in plastic containers.
- Add ginger ale at serving time.
- Garnish with fresh fruit. Should be slushy when served.

Serves 50

Freezes well. If frozen, microwave for 3 minutes before serving.

Mango Tango Smoothie

½	**cup mango, peeled and diced**
½	**cup plain nonfat yogurt**
	Crushed ice
	Sprig of fresh mint for garnish

- Place mango, yogurt and ice in blender or food processor and whirl away.
- Pour into glass and garnish with mint. You may want to add a little milk if the drink is too thick, or a little brown sugar for more depth of taste.

A Southern Tradition: 'Ice Tea'

Southerners drink 'ice tea' year-round, and have been doing so since the 19th century when ice became generally available. If you order tea in a restaurant in the South you'll get iced tea - probably sweetened, so if you want it hot or unsweetened, you'd better say so!

Teaberry Sangría

2   **cups water**
¾   **cup sugar**
1   **orange, sliced**
1   **lemon, sliced**
1   **lime, sliced**
4   **regular tea bags**
2   **cups red wine**
1   **(10 ounce) package frozen strawberries, thawed and pureed**
2   **cups lemon lime soda**

- Combine water and sugar in a saucepan; bring to a boil, stirring to dissolve sugar.
- Add orange, lemon and lime slices; boil 1 minute. Remove from heat; add tea bags.
- Cover and let stand 5 minutes. Remove tea bags; cool.
- Combine tea mixture, wine and strawberries in a pitcher; chill.
- Add lemon lime beverage, and gently stir. Serve immediately.

2 quarts

Strawberry Iced Tea Fizz

1   **pint fresh strawberries, stemmed and sliced**
½   **cup sugar**
5   **cups boiling water**
1   **orange pekoe tea bag**
1   **(12 ounce) can frozen lemonade concentrate, thawed**
1   **quart chilled sparkling water**
    Ice cubes

- In large bowl, combine strawberries and sugar; set aside.
- In another bowl, pour water over tea bag; steep 5 minutes. Discard tea bag; cool tea to room temperature.
- Stir tea into strawberry mixture along with lemonade concentrate; chill.
- To serve, stir in sparkling water; ladle over ice cubes in tall glasses. Serve with spoons.

Serves 12

Bread
and Breakfast

Bread

Breakfast

Mango Date Nut Bread

2	cups all-purpose flour
1½	cups sugar
1	teaspoon baking soda
½	teaspoon salt
½	teaspoon cinnamon
3	eggs, beaten
½	cup vegetable oil
1	teaspoon vanilla
2	cups chopped mango
½	cup chopped dates
½	cup chopped nuts

- Preheat oven to 350°.
- In medium bowl, combine flour, sugar, baking soda, salt and cinnamon.
- In small bowl, mix eggs, oil and vanilla. Stir into flour mixture.
- Fold in mango, dates and nuts. Batter will be stiff.
- Pour into 2 greased 8 inch loaf pans.
- Bake for 50 to 55 minutes.

2 loaves

Nothing compares to the aroma of freshly baked homemade bread. You could never buy a loaf of bread that is as fresh or flavorful. Making your own bread is definitely worth the extra effort.

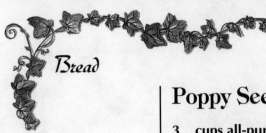

Glaze

¾ cup confectioners' sugar

½ teaspoon butter flavoring

½ teaspoon vanilla

½ teaspoon almond extract

¼ cup orange juice

• Mix sugar, butter flavoring, vanilla, almond extract and orange juice until smooth.

• Pour over cooled bread.

Poppy Seed Bread

3 cups all-purpose flour
1½ teaspoons salt
1½ teaspoons baking powder
3 eggs, beaten
1½ cups milk
¾ cup vegetable oil
2½ cups sugar
2 tablespoons poppy seeds
1½ teaspoons vanilla
1½ teaspoons almond extract
1½ teaspoons butter flavoring
  Glaze (recipe to left)

• Preheat oven to 350°.

• In large bowl, sift flour, salt and baking powder together.

• In separate bowl, cream eggs, milk, oil and sugar until batter is smooth.

• Add poppy seeds, vanilla, almond extract and butter flavoring.

• Stir in flour mixture and mix until batter is smooth.

• Pour batter into two greased and floured 9 x 5 inch loaf pans.

• Bake for 1 hour or until slightly browned.

• Remove from pans and cool on wire rack. Glaze.

2 loaves

Beverly's Dill Bread

2	cups creamed cottage cheese
2	tablespoons butter
1	tablespoon dill seed
2	tablespoons minced green onion
¼	cup sugar
¼	teaspoon baking soda
2	teaspoons salt
2	eggs, beaten
½	cup warm water
1	package dry yeast
5	cups unbleached flour

- In small pan, warm cottage cheese and butter slightly. Add dill seed, onion, sugar, baking soda, salt and eggs. Beat until blended.
- Combine water and yeast, stir and let stand until dissolved, about 5 minutes.
- Stir into cottage cheese mixture. Stir in as much of the flour as possible, then knead in the rest. Continue kneading until dough becomes smooth.
- Place dough in greased bowl, turn to grease top, cover and let stand until doubled. Punch down.
- Shape into two loaves and place in greased 8 x 4 inch loaf pans.
- Cover and let rise until dough reaches top of pans.
- Preheat oven to 375°.
- Bake 35 to 45 minutes or until browned and loaves sound hollow when tapped on the bottom. Remove from pans and cool on racks.

2 loaves

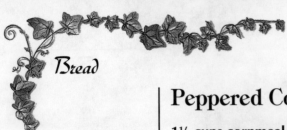

Peppered Corn Bread

Only in the South will you find cookbooks that have a special section just for cornbread recipes. Southerners are very fond of this bread no matter how it is prepared. Cornmeal can be bought plain, stone-ground or self-rising. It is made from either yellow or white corn; they can be used interchangeably. Yellow cornmeal tends to make a coarser bread.

1½ cups cornmeal
2   tablespoons all-purpose flour
2   teaspoons salt
½   teaspoon baking soda
1   cup buttermilk
¼-½ cup vegetable oil
2   eggs, beaten
1   (8 ounce) can cream-style corn
6-7 jalapeño peppers, chopped
½   bell pepper, chopped
1   large onion, chopped
2   cups grated Cheddar cheese, divided

- Preheat oven to 375°.
- In large mixing bowl, combine cornmeal, flour, salt, soda, buttermilk, oil, eggs, corn, jalapeño peppers, bell pepper and onion.
- Pour half of the mixture into a greased 9 x 13 inch baking dish; sprinkle with half of the cheese. Pour the remaining half of mixture over the first layer; add remaining cheese.
- Bake 35 minutes or until golden brown.

Serves 8 to 12

Broccoli Cornbread

1	(8½ ounce) box cornbread mix
1	(10 ounce) carton frozen, chopped broccoli, thawed and drained
1	medium onion, chopped
6	ounces cottage cheese
1	stick margarine, melted
1	teaspoon salt
4	eggs, beaten

- Preheat oven to 375°.
- In medium bowl, combine cornbread mix, broccoli, onion, cottage cheese, margarine, salt and eggs. Stir until thoroughly blended.
- Pour into a well greased 9 x 13 inch baking dish.
- Bake 35 to 45 minutes.

Serves 8 to 10

Cream Biscuits

2	cups all-purpose flour
1	teaspoon salt
1	tablespoon baking powder
2	teaspoons sugar
1	cup heavy cream
	Melted butter

- Preheat oven to 425°.
- In medium bowl, sift together flour, salt, baking powder and sugar.
- Fold in cream until a soft dough forms.
- Turn onto a floured board; knead for 1 minute.
- Pat into ¾ inch thickness. Cut into rounds, dip into melted butter.
- Place on a buttered cookie sheet and bake for 15 to 18 minutes or until slightly browned.

Serves 12

In the South, you will find biscuits gracing the table at breakfast, lunch and dinner. The most tender biscuits use solid fat such as lard or butter. A perfect biscuit should be golden brown and slightly moist inside. Biscuits can be rolled or dropped, depending on taste and time.

"Thanks to our nurses
for the wonderful
service you provided.
May God Bless all
of you."

Holiday Breakfast Bread

3   cups all-purpose flour
2   cups sugar
1   teaspoon baking soda
1   teaspoon salt
1   teaspoon cinnamon
3   eggs, beaten
1½ cups vegetable oil
1   cup chopped pecans
1   cup shredded coconut
2   cups dried bananas
1   (20 ounce) can crushed pineapple, drained
1½ teaspoons vanilla extract

- Preheat oven to 350°.
- In large mixing bowl, combine flour, sugar, soda, salt and cinnamon.
- To this mixture add eggs and oil. Mix thoroughly.
- Add pecans, coconut, bananas, pineapple and vanilla.
- Pour mixture into 2 greased loaf pans.
- Bake 1 hour to 1 hour 20 minutes until done.

2 loaves

 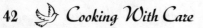

Angel Biscuits

These biscuits rise more than traditional biscuits due to the addition of yeast. They're lighter and airier.

2	packages dry yeast
¼	cup warm water
2	cups buttermilk
5	cups all-purpose flour
¼	cup sugar
1	tablespoon baking powder
1	teaspoon baking soda
1	teaspoon salt
1	cup shortening

- Preheat oven to 450°.
- Combine yeast and warm water; let stand 5 minutes. Add buttermilk to yeast mixture and set aside.
- Combine flour, sugar, baking powder, baking soda and salt in a large bowl.
- Cut in shortening with pastry blender until mixture resembles coarse meal. Add buttermilk mixture, stirring with a fork until dry ingredients are moist.
- Turn biscuit dough onto a lightly floured surface. Knead lightly 4 to 5 times.
- Roll dough to ½ inch thickness. Cut with a biscuit cutter. Place on lightly greased baking sheets. Cover and let rise in a warm place (85°) free from drafts for 1 hour.
- Bake for 10 to 12 minutes or until browned.

2 dozen

Biscuits can be made ahead and frozen. Before freezing, bake 10 minutes; cool. Place in freezer bags and freeze. To serve, remove from freezer; place biscuits on lightly greased baking sheets, and let thaw. Bake at 450° for 5 minutes or until heated.

Chive 'N' Cheddar Drop Biscuits

These biscuits may remind you of a famous seafood restaurant's biscuits.

3   cups biscuit and baking mix
1   cup finely shredded sharp Cheddar cheese
1   tablespoon chopped fresh or dried chives
½   teaspoon garlic powder
1¼ cups milk
½   cup sour cream
3   tablespoons butter, melted

- Preheat oven to 425°.
- Combine baking mix, cheese, chives and garlic powder in a large bowl; make a well in center of mixture.
- In a small bowl, combine milk and sour cream; add to baking mix mixture, stirring just until dry ingredients are moistened.
- Take ¼ cup of batter and pour onto a lightly greased baking sheet; brush with butter.
- Bake for 8 to 10 minutes or until golden.

Serves 8 to 16

Bran Muffins

12 paper liners for muffins (optional)
1½ cups milk
1½ cups raisin nut bran cereal
1½ cups biscuit and baking mix
½ cup sugar
2   tablespoons margarine
1   egg, beaten

- Preheat oven to 400°.
- Grease bottoms of 12 muffin cups or line with paper baking cups.
- In medium bowl, pour milk over cereal; let stand 2 minutes.
- Stir in biscuit mix, sugar, margarine and egg.
- Fill cups ½ to ¾ full, depending on the size muffin you desire.
- Bake 20 to 25 minutes or until golden brown and firm to touch.

9 to 12 muffins

Blueberry Muffins

1½ cups self-rising flour
½ teaspoon baking powder
1   cup sugar
¼ cup shortening
½ cup milk
1   egg, beaten
1   cup blueberries

- Preheat oven to 400°.
- In medium mixing bowl, combine flour, baking powder and sugar.
- Cut in shortening until crumbly. Add milk and egg.
- Fold in blueberries. Spoon into greased muffin cups.
- Bake 15 to 20 minutes.

18 muffins

Muffins are popular choices because there are so many variations. They can be made as breakfast food (especially for those people in a hurry) or as tasty appetizers if made smaller. The important thing to remember when making muffins is to use the right mixing technique. Combine dry ingredients in the order listed; after combining the liquid ingredients, make a well in the center of dry ingredients. Pour liquid into the well; stir just until dry ingredients are moist. Remove muffins from pans as soon as they are finished baking.

Blueberry Bran Muffins

⅓ cup butter, softened
½ cup sugar
1   egg
¾ cup milk
¼ teaspoon vanilla
1⅔ cups all-purpose flour
2½ teaspoons baking powder
½ teaspoon salt
¼ cup oat bran
1   cup blueberries

- Preheat oven to 425°.
- In medium mixing bowl, beat butter and sugar until light and fluffy.
- Add egg, milk and vanilla; mix well.
- Mix flour, baking powder, salt and oat bran; add to butter mixture.
- Stir with a fork just until blended.
- Fold in blueberries. Spoon into greased muffin pans.

12 muffins

Cheese and Ham Muffins

2   cups self-rising flour
½ teaspoon baking soda
1   cup milk
½ cup mayonnaise
½ cup cooked ham, diced
½ cup shredded Cheddar cheese

- Preheat oven to 425°.
- In a small bowl, combine flour and baking soda; set aside.
- In another bowl, combine milk, mayonnaise, ham and cheese.
- Stir into dry ingredients until moistened. Fill greased muffin tins about ⅔ full.
- Bake 16 to 18 minutes.

12 muffins

Orange Cream Cheese Muffins

1¾ cups all-purpose flour
¼ cup sugar
½ teaspoon salt
¼ cup nuts, chopped
1 egg
⅓ cup orange juice
⅓ cup orange marmalade
¼ cup milk
¼ cup oil
Orange Cream Cheese Frosting (recipe follows)

- Preheat oven to 425°.
- In small bowl, sift together flour, sugar and salt. Add nuts. Set aside.
- In small mixing bowl, combine egg, orange juice, marmalade, milk and oil.
- Add to all-purpose flour mixture; stir quickly just until dry ingredients are moistened.
- Fill greased muffin tins ⅔ full.
- Bake 20 to 25 minutes.

Orange Cream Cheese Frosting
1½ ounces cream cheese, softened
2 cups confectioners' sugar
¼ cup orange marmalade

- In small bowl, combine cream cheese, sugar and marmalade. Mix well.
- Frost muffins after they are cool.

12 muffins

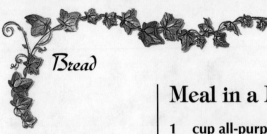

"My husband became very attached to each of his caregivers. We are so thankful to you and your willingness to share a portion of your lives with us. You became family."

Meal in a Muffin

1   cup all-purpose flour
3/4 cup whole wheat flour
1/2 cup oatmeal
1   cup sugar
1 1/2 teaspoons baking powder
1/2 teaspoon baking soda
1   teaspoon salt
1/2 cup raisins
1   cup grated carrots
1   egg, beaten
1/4 cup salad oil
1   (6 ounce) can orange juice concentrate, thawed

- Preheat oven to 400°.
- Blend all-purpose and whole wheat flours, oatmeal, sugar, baking powder, baking soda and salt.
- Add raisins and carrots; mix well.
- In small bowl, combine egg, oil and orange juice concentrate. Mix well. Combine all ingredients.
- Line muffin pan with paper liners; fill each cup with about 2/3 full.
- Bake 20 minutes.

12 muffins

Caramel Breakfast Rolls

1½ packages frozen yeast rolls
½   cup brown sugar
½   cup butter
1   (6 ounce) package butterscotch pudding (not instant)
**   Cinnamon to taste**
1   cup chopped pecans

- Preheat oven to 350°.
- Place rolls in greased, 11 x 7 inch baking dish.
- In small pan, cook sugar and butter just long enough to dissolve sugar.
- Pour over rolls.
- Sprinkle pudding, cinnamon and pecans over rolls.
- Let rise overnight.
- Bake rolls for 20 to 30 minutes.

Serves 8 to 10

French Breakfast Puffs

1   cup sugar, divided
1   egg
⅓ cup shortening
1½ cups sifted all-purpose flour
1½ teaspoons baking powder
½ teaspoon salt
¼ teaspoon ground nutmeg
½ cup milk
1   teaspoon ground cinnamon
**   Melted butter**

- Preheat oven to 350°.
- With mixer, cream ½ cup sugar, egg and shortening.
- Sift together flour, baking powder, salt and nutmeg.
- Add creamed mixture alternately with milk, beating well after each addition.
- Fill 12 greased muffin pans ⅔ full with batter.
- Bake 20 to 25 minutes.
- When removed from oven, dip puffs, while still hot, in melted butter and roll in mixture of cinnamon and remaining sugar.

Serves 12

Freezes well. Serve hot or cold.

Overnight Blueberry French Toast

This is a very unique breakfast dish. Good for any holiday breakfast or brunch. It's filled with the fresh taste of blueberries and covered with a rich blueberry sauce to make this one of a kind.

12 slices day-old bread
2 (8 ounce) packages cream cheese
1 cup blueberries
12 eggs
2 cups milk
1 teaspoon vanilla extract
¹/₃ cup maple syrup or honey
   Blueberry sauce (recipe to right)

- Grease 9 x 13 inch baking dish and set aside.
- Cut bread into 1 inch cubes; place half into prepared dish. Cut cream cheese into 1 inch cubes and place over bread. Top with blueberries and remaining bread cubes.
- Beat eggs in large bowl; add milk, vanilla and syrup or honey. Mix well; pour over bread cubes. Cover and refrigerate overnight. Next morning, remove from the refrigerator ¹/₂ hour before baking.
- Preheat oven to 350°.
- Cover and bake for 30 minutes. Remove cover and bake another 25 to 30 minutes or until center is set and is golden in color.

Blueberry Sauce

1 cup sugar
2 tablespoons cornstarch
1 cup water
1 cup blueberries
1 tablespoon butter

- In small saucepan, combine sugar and cornstarch. Add water and bring to a boil over medium heat; stir constantly and boil for 3 to 4 minutes.
- Stir in blueberries and reduce heat; simmer for 10 minutes or until blueberries pop. Stir in the butter and pour over French Toast.

Serves 8 to 10

French toast is probably the easiest of breakfast foods; especially the version that sits overnight and is ready to cook as soon as you get out of bed. It can bake while you get showered and dressed.

Baked French Toast

1	loaf French bread
6	large eggs, slightly beaten
1½	cups milk
1	cup half-and-half
1	teaspoon vanilla
¼	teaspoon ground cinnamon
¼	teaspoon ground nutmeg
¼	cup softened butter
½	cup brown sugar
¼	cup chopped walnuts
1	tablespoon light corn syrup

- The night before using - cut bread into 1½ inch slices and place in 9 x 13 inch dish or individual baking dishes.
- Mix together eggs, milk, half-and-half, vanilla, cinnamon and nutmeg. Spoon over bread; cover and refrigerate overnight.
- Preheat oven to 325°.
- Combine butter, brown sugar, walnuts and corn syrup. Sprinkle evenly over bread slices.
- Bake 45 minutes or until golden brown.
- Serve with your favorite syrup.

Serves 6 to 10

Multi Grain Pancake Mix

½ **cup oatmeal**
2 **cups all-purpose flour**
½ **cup whole wheat flour**
½ **cup cornmeal**
¼ **cup unprocessed wheat bran**
¼ **cup toasted wheat germ**
¼ **cup sugar**
2 **teaspoons baking powder**
1½ **teaspoons salt**
1 **teaspoon baking soda**

• Place oatmeal in processor and process until smooth. Add all-purpose flour, wheat flour, cornmeal, wheat bran, wheat germ, sugar, baking powder, salt and baking soda. Process until smooth. Store in tightly covered container in refrigerator.

4 cups mixture

Pancakes

1 cup buttermilk
3 tablespoons vegetable oil
2 egg whites, lightly beaten
1½ cups multi grain pancake mix

• Combine buttermilk, oil and egg whites in medium bowl; mix well. Add pancake mix and stir just until blended. Using about ¼ cup batter, fry on hot griddle.

Overnight Raisin Oatmeal Pancakes

2	**cups quick cooking oats**
2	**cups buttermilk**
2	**eggs, beaten**
¼	**cup butter, softened**
⅓	**cup raisins**
½	**cup all-purpose flour**
2	**tablespoons white sugar**
1	**teaspoon baking powder**
1	**teaspoon baking soda**
½	**teaspoon ground cinnamon**
½	**teaspoon salt**

Pancake mixes may save a little time in the kitchen, but they are much better when made from scratch. The flavor and texture of the homemade versions are well worth the effort, especially when you have guests. If in doubt as to when to turn pancakes, just remember, the top is full of bubbles and edges are somewhat brown. The second side will take only a minute.

- In a medium mixing bowl, mix together the oatmeal and buttermilk. Cover and refrigerate overnight.
- The next morning, add the eggs, butter and raisins to oat mixture. Mix well.
- Sift together the flour, sugar, baking powder, baking soda, cinnamon and salt. Add oatmeal mixture and stir to moisten. Allow batter to sit 20 minutes before cooking.
- Pour ¼ cup batter on hot griddle for each cake. If batter is too thick, add buttermilk, 1 tablespoon at a time until desired consistency. Cook cakes until bubbles appear on top; turn to brown.

Serves 18

Waffles

1	**egg**
¼	**cup vegetable oil**
1	**cup buttermilk**
¼	**teaspoon baking soda**
1	**cup all-purpose flour**
¼	**teaspoon salt**
1	**heaping teaspoon baking powder**
½	**tablespoon sugar**

- Put egg, oil and buttermilk into blender.
- Add baking soda, flour, salt, baking powder and sugar; mix well on low speed.
- Pour from blender onto hot waffle iron and cook about 3 minutes.
- Spray with non-stick cooking spray between each waffle.

6 waffles

When you have leftover waffles, freeze for up to 1 month. These waffles can be toasted and taste just as fresh as when you made them. Use leftover waffles when you're serving creamed meat or vegetable sauces. You can also top them with ice cream and fruit toppings. You may want to make a double batch just so you always have some ready.

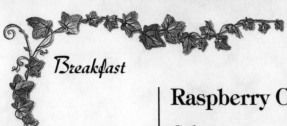

Raspberry Cream Cheese Coffee Cake

Cake

2¼ cups all-purpose flour
¾   cup sugar
¾   cup butter or margarine
½   teaspoon baking powder
½   teaspoon baking soda
½   teaspoon salt
¾   cup sour cream
1   egg
1   teaspoon almond extract
    Topping (recipe follows)

- Preheat oven to 350°.
- Grease and flour the bottom and sides of a 9 inch or 10 inch springform pan.
- In a mixing bowl, combine flour and sugar. Mix well.
- Add butter or margarine and blend until mixture resembles coarse crumbs.
- Measure out 1 cup of the crumb mixture and set aside.
- To remaining crumb mixture, add baking powder, baking soda, salt, sour cream, egg and extract. Blend well.
- Spread batter over the bottom and 2 inches up the sides of prepared pan. (Batter should be about ¼ inch thick on sides.)

Topping

1   (8 ounce) package cream cheese, softened
¼   cup sugar
1   egg
½   cup raspberry preserves
½   cup sliced almonds

- In small bowl, combine cream cheese, sugar and egg. Blend well.
- Pour over batter in pan.
- Carefully spoon preserves over cream cheese filling.

Raspberry Cream Cheese Coffee Cake *continued*

- Add almonds to reserved crumb mixture. Sprinkle over top of cake.
- Bake for 45 to 55 minutes or until cream cheese filling is set and crust is deep golden brown. Cool 15 minutes before removing sides of pan.

Serves 12

True Grit

The Ten Commandments of Grits

1. Thou shalt not put syrup on thy grits.

2. Thou shalt not eat thy grits with a spoon.

3. Thou shalt not eat cream of wheat and call it grits for this is blasphemy.

4. Thou shalt not covet thy neighbors grits.

5. Thou shalt only use salt, butter and cheese as toppings for thy grits. Lose the milk.

6. Thou shalt not eat instant grits!

7. Thou shalt not put syrup or sugar on thy grits.

8. Thou shalt not put syrup or sugar on thy grits.

9. Thou shalt not put syrup or sugar on thy grits.

10. Thou shalt not enjoy grits for breakfast only! They're good any time.

Grits Breakfast Casserole

This recipe can be made ahead and frozen. Freeze uncooked.
Thaw in refrigerator and cook according to baking directions.

2 **pounds sausage (hot or regular)**
1 **cup raw grits, cooked**
2 **cups shredded sharp Cheddar cheese**
½ **stick butter**
5 **eggs**
1½ **cups milk**
Salt and pepper to taste

• Preheat oven to 350°.

• Brown and drain sausage; crumble in bottom of a 9 x 13 inch greased casserole dish.

• Cook grits according to package directions (stiff is better than runny).

• Add cheese and butter to grits; stir well.

• In mixing bowl, beat eggs, milk, salt and pepper together. Add to slightly cooled grits mixture.

• Pour over sausage in casserole.

• Bake for 1 hour uncovered.

Serves 12 to 16

There is no such thing as a "Grit Tree". Southerners like to hide a smile when a Northern friend wants to know where grits grow. Grits are coarsely ground corn or hominy cooked as a cereal or a side dish to the southern breakfast. In the South, grits are a must. Grits have become increasingly popular in upscale restaurants. There are several "Grits Cookbooks" that have become very popular.

Chicken Quiche

1 (9 inch) pie crust
1½ cups cooked chicken, boned and diced
1 small onion, chopped
½ pound Cheddar cheese, shredded
½ pound Swiss cheese, shredded
4 eggs, beaten
1 cup milk
1 cup half-and-half
   Salt and pepper to taste

- Preheat oven to 450°.
- Place chicken into pie crust.
- Top with onion, Cheddar cheese and Swiss cheese.
- In small bowl, mix eggs, milk, half-and-half, salt and pepper; pour over chicken mixture.
- Bake 15 minutes. Reduce heat to 350° and bake for 20 minutes longer.

Serves 6 to 8

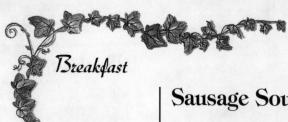

"A special thanks to the chaplain - he was wonderful and the special Christmas carolers were so beautiful. No - you all do not leave us alone, God's inner love has been expressed through you."

Sausage Soufflé

1	pound mild sausage
5	eggs
1	pint milk
1	pint half-and-half
1	cup Cheddar cheese, shredded
1	teaspoon paprika
1	teaspoon Worcestershire sauce
1	teaspoon garlic salt
1	teaspoon dry mustard
	Butter
12	slices soft, buttered bread - trim crust

- Preheat oven to 350°.
- Brown sausage in small skillet; drain and crumble.
- In large bowl, combine eggs, milk, half-and-half, cheese, paprika, Worcestershire sauce, garlic salt and mustard. Mix until well blended. Add sausage and stir.
- Cut bread into small pieces; line bottom of 9 x 13 inch greased baking dish with bread.
- Pour egg mixture over bread.
- Bake 1 hour.

Serves 6 to 8

Ham and Cheese Casserole

16 slices white bread, divided
1 pound boiled ham, chopped
½ pound Swiss cheese, cubed
¼ pound sharp Cheddar cheese, grated
6 eggs, beaten
3 cups milk
1 teaspoon salt
1 teaspoon onion salt
1 teaspoon dry mustard
2 cups crushed cornflakes
⅓ cup melted butter

- Butter or spray 9 x 13 inch baking dish.
- Remove crust from bread. Place 8 slices on bottom to cover.
- Combine ham and cheeses and place on bread.
- Place remaining 8 slices of bread on top.
- Combine eggs, milk, salt, onion salt and dry mustard.
- Pour over top.
- Refrigerate overnight (covered).
- Preheat oven to 375°.
- Mix cornflake crumbs and butter. Sprinkle over bread layer.
- Bake for 45 minutes uncovered. Let stand 10 minutes before cutting into squares.

Serves 10 to 12

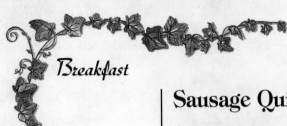

Sausage Quiche

1   (9 inch) deep dish pie shell
1   pound sausage
1   medium onion, chopped
3   eggs, beaten
⅔   cup milk
1   teaspoon salt
4-5 dashes cayenne pepper
1½ cups shredded Cheddar cheese

- Bake pie shell 3 minutes at 400°. Remove and prick with fork; bake another 5 minutes. Turn oven to 375°.
- In skillet, brown sausage; add onion and fry until tender. Drain fat.
- Combine eggs, milk, salt and pepper. Mix well. Stir in sausage.
- Sprinkle half of the cheese over the bottom of pie crust. Add egg and sausage mixture. Top with remaining cheese.
- Bake at 375° for 50 minutes. Cool about 10 minutes before serving.

Serves 6

Soups and Salads

Soups

Salads

Roasted Butternut Soup

1   **medium butternut squash**
8   **tablespoons butter, divided**
1   **large yellow onion, chopped**
4   **cups chicken broth**
½   **cup whipping cream**
    Salt and white pepper to taste

- Peel squash and cut the top part. Discard seeds and cut squash into large cubes.
- In large pot, melt 4 tablespoons butter; add the onion and cook until translucent. Add squash, cooking on low temperature about 5 minutes.
- Add broth and simmer about 45 minutes.
- Scoop squash from shell (it will come out in large chunks). Add to broth. Blend mixture until smooth with hand blender.
- Puree the soup (strain if you want a very velvety soup) and add cream. Bring to a boil and add remaining butter. Add salt and pepper and simmer for 10 minutes to allow flavors to meld.

Serves 8

Soups offer more variety to menu planning than almost any other type food. Add to a sandwich or salad and you have a complete meal. A hearty soup and French bread make a delightful meal on cold winter evenings. They can be casual enough to serve at the family meal or formal enough to serve as a first course for an elegant dinner. There are hearty soups to serve on cold, blustery days or chilled soups that are perfect on a hot summer day. Take note of the season and your mood, and then choose the soup.

Fresh Green Pea Soup

¾ cup chopped onion
2   tablespoons butter
1½ cups green peas, fresh or frozen
2½ cups chicken broth
1   cup milk
2   tablespoons flour
    Salt and pepper to taste
⅓ cup buttermilk

- Sauté onion and butter.
- Add green peas and chicken broth. Simmer until tender.
- Add milk, flour, salt and pepper. Simmer about 10 minutes.
- Add buttermilk and heat but do not boil.
- May be served with toasted French bread.

Serves 6 to 8

Creamy Fresh Vegetable Soup

¼ **cup vegetable oil**
2   **cups small cauliflower florets**
1   **cup carrots sliced in 1-inch match sticks**
1   **cup celery, thinly sliced**
2   **cups chicken broth**
¼ **cup flour**
¾ **cup milk**
½ **teaspoon salt**
¼ **teaspoon ground black pepper**
¼ **teaspoon ground nutmeg**

- In a medium saucepan, heat oil until hot. Add cauliflower, carrots and celery. Cook and stir until tender, about 10 minutes.
- In a small bowl, combine chicken broth and flour. Add to saucepan, stirring constantly over high heat, until slightly thickened, about 2 to 3 minutes.
- Add milk, salt, pepper and nutmeg.
- Cook until just hot.

Serves 6 to 8

Hot or cold, thick or thin, vegetable soups have always played an important role in Southern menus. They're a great way of getting rid of leftovers. When making vegetable soup, remember to take into consideration that all vegetables do not cook in the same length of time. Vegetables that take the longest to cook should be added first.

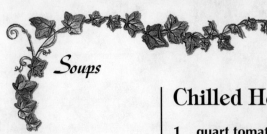

Chilled Herb and Tomato Soup

This recipe came from The Bakery Lane Soup Bowl in Middleburg, VT. It is great to take on picnics in a thermos bottle. Serve in pretty cups or glasses. Salad and sandwiches complete the meal.

1	**quart tomato juice**
¼	**cup salad oil**
¼	**cup vinegar**
½	**cup milk**
2	**tablespoons lemon juice**
1	**clove garlic, minced**
2	**tablespoons sugar**
1	**teaspoon dry mustard**
1	**tablespoon fresh rosemary, chopped**
1	**tablespoon basil, dried**
1	**teaspoon thyme, dried**
	Salt and pepper to taste
	Chopped and peeled cucumber (optional)

- Combine tomato juice, oil and vinegar.
- Beat in milk and lemon juice.
- Add garlic, sugar, dry mustard, rosemary, basil, thyme, salt and pepper.
- Chill at least 24 hours.
- Strain to remove herbs or blend in small batches.
- Serve soup with cucumbers if desired.

Serves 5

Crab Bisque

1   celery rib, thinly sliced
1   small onion, chopped
½   cup green pepper, chopped
3   tablespoons butter or margarine
2   (14¾ ounce) cans cream style corn
2   (10¾ ounce) cans condensed cream of potato soup, undiluted
1   cup milk
1½ cups half-and-half
2   bay leaves (discard after cooking)
1   teaspoon thyme, dried
½   teaspoon garlic powder
¼   teaspoon white pepper
⅛   teaspoon hot pepper sauce
3   (6 ounce) cans crabmeat drained and flaked
    (remove cartilage)

• In a large saucepan or soup kettle, sauté celery, onion, and
  green pepper in melted butter until tender.
• Add corn, potato soup, milk, half-and-half, bay leaves, thyme,
  garlic powder, white pepper, hot pepper sauce and mix well.
  Stir in crab, heat thoroughly but do not boil.

Serves 12

Barley Mushroom Soup

½ cup barley, uncooked
6½ cups water, divided
2   tablespoons butter or margarine
1   cup chopped onion
1-2 cloves garlic, minced
1½ pounds mushrooms, sliced thin
     Salt and pepper to taste
3   tablespoons soy sauce
3   tablespoons cooking sherry

- Place barley and 1½ cups water in large saucepan. Bring to boil, cover and simmer about 20 to 30 minutes.
- While barley is cooking, melt butter in skillet. Add onion and sauté about 5 minutes.
- Add garlic, mushrooms, salt and pepper.
- Cover and cook until tender, about 10 minutes. Stir occasionally.
- Add soy sauce and sherry.
- Combine mushroom mixture with the barley and remaining 5 cups water.
- Partially cover pan and gently simmer about 15 minutes.

Serves 8

Cold Cantaloupe Soup

1	**medium cantaloupe, cubed**
2	**medium peaches, diced**
¼	**cup orange juice**
¼	**cup light rum**
1	**tablespoon honey**
½	**cup orange zest (divided)**
1	**(8 ounce) carton plain yogurt**

- Combine cantaloupe, peaches, orange juice, rum, honey and ¼ cup orange zest.
- Pour into processor or blender. Process until mixture is smooth.
- Pour into large glass bowl. Cover with plastic wrap.
- Chill at least 4 hours.
- Ladle into chilled soup bowls and top with yogurt and remaining ¼ cup orange zest.

Serves 8

Be creative when serving soups. Pick out your best mugs and serve a steaming bowl of chili in front of the fireplace. Sip cold soups from chilled wine glasses or punch cups. At a formal dinner party, serve cold soups in a small glass cup nested in a larger bowl filled with ice.

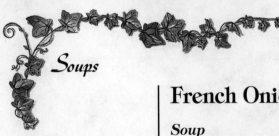

Keep the garnishes for soup simple. Chopped herbs or green onions add a touch of color to just about any soup; croutons offer a little crunch. Grated Parmesan cheese, finely diced egg white or perhaps a thin slice of lemon will add just the right touch of color.

French Onion Soup

Soup

6	cups thinly sliced Vidalia onions (or other sweet onion)
4	tablespoons butter
2	tablespoons oil
1	teaspoon salt
½	teaspoon sugar
3	tablespoons flour
2	quarts canned beef broth, boiling hot
½	cup dry white wine
	Salt and pepper to taste

- Slowly cook onions in butter and oil in large, heavy, covered saucepan 15 minutes. Uncover, raise heat to medium and stir in salt and sugar. Cook for 35 to 40 minutes, stirring frequently, until onions are golden brown.
- Sprinkle in flour and stir for 2 minutes.
- Add boiling broth all at once and stir until slightly thickened and smooth.
- Add wine, salt and pepper. Simmer partially covered for 30 minutes, skimming occasionally.

Finishing Touches

1	tablespoon grated onion
12-16	(1-inch thick) slices hard-toasted French bread
1½	cups freshly grated mozzarella cheese
1	tablespoon olive oil

- Preheat oven to 325°. Bring soup to a boil and pour into individual flame and oven-proof soup mugs. Stir in grated onion. Float toast rounds on top of the soup and sprinkle with grated cheese. Drizzle with oil and bake for 20 minutes. Broil for a few seconds to brown the top and serve immediately.

Serves 6 to 8

Chicken and Wild Rice Soup

¼ **cup butter**
1 **cup sliced, fresh mushrooms**
1 **cup chopped onion**
1 **cup diced celery**
⅓ **cup flour**
6 **cups chicken broth**
4 **cooked chicken breasts, chopped**
2 **cups cooked wild rice**
1 **cup half-and-half**
2 **tablespoons dry white wine**

- Melt butter, add mushrooms and cook about 5 minutes.
- Add onions and celery and cook about 10 minutes.
- Add flour, stirring constantly. Cook about 5 minutes.
- Add chicken broth and stir until mixture thickens.
- Add chicken and rice. Bring to boiling point but do not boil.
- Turn heat to low.
- Add half-and-half and stir until warm.
- Add wine and stir well.

Serves 6

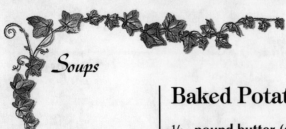

Baked Potato Soup

¼ **pound butter (do not use margarine)**
1 **quart diced onions**
½ **cup flour**
2 **quarts chicken stock**
1¼ **cups potato buds**
1 **quart half-and-half**
   Salt and pepper to taste
1 **teaspoon basil**
   Dash Tabasco sauce
3 **cups baked, diced potatoes**
8 **ounces shredded Monterey Jack cheese (optional)**

- Sauté butter and onions on low 10 to 15 minutes. Do not brown.
- Add flour to onions and cook 4 to 5 minutes. Do not brown.
- Mix chicken stock and potato buds with a whisk. Blend until smooth.
- Add stock mixture to roux mixing slowly with whisk.
- Cook 15 to 20 minutes. (May refrigerate at this point if preparing ahead)
- Stir in half-and-half. Cook for 10 minutes. Do not bring to boil!
- Season with salt, pepper, basil and Tabasco sauce.
- Add potatoes.
- Sprinkle each bowl with cheese if desired.

Serves 10 to 12

 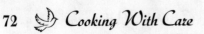

Cream of Mushroom Soup

*Substitute broccoli if you would prefer Cream of Broccoli Soup.
Either way is delicious.*

4   tablespoons butter
1   pound mushrooms, chopped fine (or broccoli)
4   tablespoons flour
4   cups chicken stock - boiling hot
    Salt, pepper, onion juice, cayenne to taste
1   cup heavy cream
    Parsley for garnish

- Melt butter in a heavy pot. Add mushrooms (or broccoli) and stir to coat well.
- Add the flour through a strainer, stirring well.
- Let this mixture bubble for the flour must cook. Do not let it brown.
- Add chicken stock, stirring rapidly.
- Cover pan and cook over medium heat until steam emerges from under the lid.
- Remove the lid and simmer 8 minutes.
- Add seasonings, stirring well.
- Add cream and bring to a bare simmer.
- Sprinkle with parsley and serve hot.

Serves 6 to 8

"Mother would talk to me about how nice the chaplain was and how much she enjoyed his visits and prayers. Thank you."

Corn Chowder

6-8 potatoes, peeled and diced
2   (1 pound) bags frozen cream style corn
1   stick butter
1   quart half-and-half
2-3 cups milk
½   tablespoon dried rosemary
    Grated Cheddar cheese
    Crumbled bacon

- Boil potatoes until tender; drain.
- Add corn, butter, half-and-half, milk and rosemary. Simmer about ½ hour.
- Serve with grated cheese and bacon.

Serves 8

Broccoli Cheddar Chowder

3   cups water
1   (14.5 ounce) can chicken broth
5   potatoes, cubed
1   (10 ounce) box frozen chopped broccoli
3   cups milk
½   cup all-purpose flour
8   tablespoons butter
1   cup shredded sharp Cheddar cheese
1½ pounds processed cheese loaf

- Combine water, chicken broth and potatoes. Cook potatoes until soft. During last 5 minutes, add broccoli.
- In separate pan, combine milk, flour and butter until melted.
- Add Cheddar and processed cheese; stir to melt.
- Add cheese mixture to potatoes and broccoli.
- Simmer on very low heat until soup has thickened. (You may use more potatoes and more cheese to suit your taste.)

Serves 8 to 10

Abbeville's Historic Trinity Episcopal Church

Aptly described as "a mellow gem of Gothic architecture in a setting of fragrant boxwood gardens and magnificent old magnolias", Trinity Church in Abbeville is an historic and spiritual landmark of the Upcountry. The Episcopal Church, once the town's principal denomination, dates from 1842. In that year a Charleston barrister, Thomas Parker, moved with his family to the prosperous farming area and erected a small frame church building near the town square. George Walker of Columbia avoided flamboyance in his design for Trinity church. With modified Gothic elements he created a traditional and chastely beautiful building which evokes the architecture of older Western European churches. Trinity Church, including its bell and rare John Baker organ, both still in use, was constructed for $16,655.

Canadian Cheese Soup

2   **tablespoons butter**
½   **cup very finely diced onion**
½   **cup very finely diced celery**
½   **cup very finely diced carrot**
1   **cup chicken broth**
2   **tablespoons all-purpose flour**
3   **cups milk, divided**
2   **cups shredded white sharp Cheddar cheese**
⅛   **teaspoon paprika**
¼   **teaspoon Tabasco sauce**
     Salt and white pepper to taste
     Parsley for garnish (optional)

- Melt butter in large saucepan; add onion, celery and carrot. Cook gently stirring often (about 10 minutes) until vegetables soften. Add chicken broth and stir. Cover and simmer 15 minutes.
- Put flour into 2 cup measure and add a little milk; mix thoroughly and fill to 2 cup mark, stirring until blended.
- Add to soup; heat and stir until boiling and thickened.
- Add cheese, paprika, Tabasco sauce, salt and pepper.
- Let set, off heat. When ready to serve, add remaining 1 cup milk and more chicken broth to taste. Reheat to just below boiling point before serving.
- Sprinkle with parsley. Serve with garlic toast points.

Serves 4 to 6

Caesar Salad

Romaine lettuce is a long-leafed head with coarse, crisp leaves and heavy ribs. Usually the leaves are torn into bite-size pieces, and the tough ribs discarded.

Croutons

1½ tablespoons unsalted butter
1½ tablespoons virgin olive oil
3 cloves garlic, minced
½ loaf French bread, cubed

- Melt butter and oil in sauté pan.
- Sauté garlic over medium heat until browned.
- Remove garlic from pan. In the seasoned oil/butter mixture, sauté bread cubes, stirring constantly until coated and brown.
- Finish in oven for 5 minutes at 350°.

Salad
1	**large head romaine lettuce**
	Dressing (recipe follows)

- Wash and dry lettuce thoroughly. Tear into bite-size pieces.

Dressing
¼	**teaspoon anchovy paste**
1	**large garlic clove, crushed**
1	**teaspoon Dijon mustard**
2	**dashes Worcestershire sauce**
1	**egg yolk**
1	**lemon, juiced**
5	**tablespoons freshly grated Parmesan cheese, divided**
	Salt and ground pepper to taste

- Mash anchovy paste and garlic in bottom of large salad bowl.
- Mix in mustard, Worcestershire sauce, egg yolk and blend well.
- Add lemon juice (dressing should be consistency of very thin liquid).
- Add 3 tablespoons Parmesan cheese slowly, stirring constantly, so that dressing thickens to a thin paste.
- Add salt and pepper.

Serves 4 to 6

Greek Salad

2   pounds tomatoes, coarsely chopped
1   cup sliced onion
1   cup cucumber, coarsely chopped
½   cup black olives
¾   cup coarsely diced bell pepper
     Dressing (recipe follows)

• Combine tomatoes, onion, cucumber, black olives and bell pepper in a medium bowl.

Dressing
¼   cup red wine vinegar
½   cup olive oil
¼   teaspoon dried oregano
¼   teaspoon dried basil
½   pound feta cheese, diced
     Salt and fresh ground pepper to taste

• Combine vinegar, oil, oregano, basil together.
• Pour over vegetables and stir gently.
• Add salt, pepper and cheese.
• Chill well.

Serves 6

Due West of What?

This is the question most commonly asked when referring to the town of Due West. It is located in an area rich in colonial, Revolutionary, and antebellum history. In this area, important treaties were signed with the Cherokee nation opening Indian lands to white settlers. Prior to the Cherokee War, Long Cane Creek was the boundary between the Cherokee Nation and the Province of South Carolina. What is now northern Abbeville County, belonged to the Cherokee nation. In the first years of the American Revolution, South Carolina dealt the Cherokees a series of defeats, and in 1777 at "Dewitts" or "DeWisse's" Corner, six miles northwest of the current town of Due West, the Cherokees signed a peace treaty ceding South Carolina

Scandinavian Salad

This salad gets better the longer it is kept.

1 **(16 ounce) can tiny green peas with pearl onions**
1 **(16 ounce) can French cut green beans**
1 **(4 ounce) jar chopped pimento**
1 **teaspoon dehydrated onion, soaked 5 minutes in water**
3 **ribs celery, chopped fine**
   Dressing (recipe follows)

• Drain peas, green beans and pimento and combine with onion and celery.

½ **cup white vinegar**
½ **cup sugar**
½ **cup salad oil**

• Combine vinegar, sugar and oil until well blended.
• Pour over vegetable mixture and mix carefully.
• Let stand at least 12 hours in refrigerator before serving.

Serves 6 to 8

Romaine Orange Almond Salad

The sugared almonds are well worth the effort.

Salad

2   quarts romaine, torn
1   (20 ounce) can Mandarin oranges, drained
1½   cups chopped celery
3   tablespoons chopped green onion
½   cup sliced almonds
3   tablespoons sugar
      Dressing (recipe follows)

- At serving time, combine romaine, oranges, celery, green onion and sugared almonds.
- Make sugared almonds by carefully cooking sugar and almonds over medium heat in a small skillet, stirring constantly until sugar is dissolved and almonds are coated. Almonds burn easily so watch very carefully.
- Store almonds in an airtight container until you are ready to use them.

Dressing

⅓   cup salad oil
2½   tablespoons sugar
2½   tablespoons vinegar
½   teaspoon salt
      Dash almond extract

- Combine oil, sugar, vinegar, salt and almond extract. Blend thoroughly.
- Refrigerate dressing 2 hours before mixing salad. After salad is mixed, pour dressing on and toss to coat.

Serves 8 to 10

that part of the state now known as Pickens, Oconee, Anderson and Greenville Counties. It is believed that the original name of the town, "Due West Corner", was derived from the name "DeWits Corner".

Bibb lettuce is a small, cup-shaped head of lettuce with deep green veins. The veins and ribs of Bibb are less prominent than in other lettuces, which gives it a softer texture. It adds a unique taste to salads. Boston is similar in looks, taste and texture to Bibb but is larger. Green and red leaf lettuce have delicate leaves that grow loosely rather than in heads like iceberg; the leaves are clustered only at the core. Most leaf lettuce is medium green; red-leafed varieties have curly red-tipped edges. Leaf lettuce is crisp when cold; it should be used soon after it's purchased.

Brie and Blueberry Salad

2　tablespoons black currant vinegar
2　teaspoons fresh lemon juice
4　tablespoons hazelnut oil
4　tablespoons light vegetable oil
　　Pinch ground nutmeg
　　Salt and freshly ground pepper to taste
4　cups torn Bibb or Boston lettuce
4　cups torn red-leaf lettuce
2　tablespoons small fresh mint leaves
½　pint fresh blueberries (about 1 cup)
8　thin slices (about 4 ounces) Brie

- In small bowl, whisk together vinegar, lemon juice, hazelnut oil, vegetable oil and nutmeg. Season with salt and pepper; whisk until well blended.

- In a large salad bowl, toss lettuces and mint leaves with just enough dressing to coat them lightly. Divide greens among 8 chilled salad plates.

- Scatter about 2 tablespoons blueberries over each salad, and arrange a slice of cheese in center of each salad. Serve immediately.

Serves 8

If cheese is reasonably firm, chop it into pieces the size of the berries; if very soft, put a single portion in the center of each salad.

Spinach Salad with Blueberry Vinaigrette

Salad

1   pound fresh, baby spinach leaves, washed
2-3 pears, washed and sliced
1   cup fresh blueberries
     Bleu cheese, crumbled
     Blueberry vinaigrette (Recipe follows)

• On cold salad plates, mound spinach leaves, slices of pear and blueberries.
• Sprinkle blue cheese on top.
• Drizzle with blueberry vinaigrette.

Dressing

1   part blueberry balsamic vinegar (Recipe follows)
3   parts salad oil
     Sugar optional (for less tart dressing)
     Dry Italian Salad dressing to taste

• Combine vinegar, salad oil, sugar (if desired), and dressing mix. Shake well.

Blueberry Balsamic Vinegar

4   cups frozen, thawed or fresh blueberries
1   quart balsamic vinegar
¼   cup sugar
     Lime peel cut in strips from 1 lime (green part only)
1   (3-inch) cinnamon stick

• In large non-reactive saucepan, crush blueberries with potato masher or back of a heavy spoon. Add vinegar, sugar, lime and cinnamon; bring to a boil. Reduce heat and simmer covered for 20 minutes.
• Cool slightly; pour into a large bowl. Cover and refrigerate 2 days to allow flavors to blend.
• Place wire mesh strainer over a large bowl. In batches, ladle blueberry mixture into strainer, pressing out as much liquid as possible. Discard solids.
• Pour vinegar into clean glass bottles or jars; refrigerate, tightly covered.

5½ cups

Napa (also known as Chinese cabbage) grows in slender tight heads. It has a very mild flavor. The crisper drawer in your refrigerator is the best place for greens.

Oriental Salad

Salad

½   **cup salad oil (Canola)**
2   **packages ramen noodles - crumbled**
2   **tablespoons sesame seeds**
1   **cup slivered almonds**
1   **large head Chinese cabbage (napa), shredded**
1   **bunch green onions, chopped**

- Sauté noodles, sesame seeds and almonds in oil until browned evenly. Stir frequently.
- Combine cabbage and green onions.
- Set aside.

Dressing

¼   **cup rice wine vinegar**
⅓   **cup sugar**
2   **tablespoons soy sauce**

- Bring vinegar, sugar and soy sauce to a boil.
- Let cool for 1 minute.
- Mix sautéed ingredients with cabbage and green onions.
- Pour dressing over salad and mix well.

Serves 8

Frozen Slaw

Slaw

1   **medium head cabbage, shredded coarsely**
1   **large carrot, shredded finer than cabbage**
1   **green pepper, chopped**
1   **tablespoon salt**
1   **small onion, chopped**
    Dressing (recipe follows)

- Mix cabbage and carrot with 1 tablespoon salt and let sit for 1 hour.
- Drain some of the liquid off leaving enough to moisten.
- Add green pepper and onion.

Dressing

1   **cup white vinegar**
½   **cup water**
2   **cups sugar**
1   **tablespoon mustard seeds**
1   **teaspoon celery seeds**

- Bring vinegar, water, sugar, mustard and celery seeds to a boil.
- Let cool completely.
- Pour over cabbage mixture and stir thoroughly.
- Pack in containers and freeze.
- To serve, thaw in refrigerator.

Serves 6 to 8

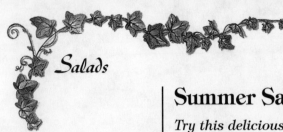

Summer Salad

Try this delicious salad when strawberries are at their peak.

Salad

1   **bunch romaine lettuce**

3-4 **cups fresh strawberries, washed, hulled and sliced**

2   **medium Vidalia onions (or other sweet onion) sliced into thin rings**

1   **cup pecans or walnuts, coarsely chopped**

     Dressing (recipe follows)

- Rinse lettuce under cold water and tear into bite-size pieces. Place in a large salad bowl.
- Add strawberries, onions, and pecans or walnuts and mix well.

Dressing

1½ **cups sugar**

⅓   **cup lemon juice**

1   **teaspoon celery seed**

1   **teaspoon dry mustard**

1   **teaspoon paprika**

½   **teaspoon salt**

¾   **cup salad oil (Do not use olive oil)**

- Mix sugar and lemon juice. Add celery seed, mustard, paprika and salt.
- Whisk while slowly adding salad oil.
- Continue beating with whisk until the oil is blended thoroughly.
- Pour over salad and toss well.

Serves 8

Erskine College

The ARP Church had high educational standards for its ministers. Because travel to such northern institutions as "Transylvania, KY, Jefferson, PA and Miami, OH was difficult, the Synod of the South established a classical school in 1836 at Due West Corner. A professor of theology was added in 1837, marking the beginning of Erskine Theological Seminary. In 1839 the curriculum was expanded and Erskine became South Carolina's first four-year denominational college. By the time of the Civil War, Erskine had become one of the thriving institutions of the South.

Harvey House Slaw

Slaw
1	head cabbage, slivered
1	large green pepper sliced in rings
2	medium Spanish onions, sliced in rings
1	cup sugar

- In a large bowl, make layers of cabbage, green peppers and onion.
- Sprinkle sugar over top.

Dressing
1	teaspoon dry mustard
2	teaspoons sugar
1	teaspoon celery salt
1	teaspoon celery seed
1	tablespoon salt
1	cup white vinegar
¾	cup salad oil

- In a saucepan, combine dry mustard, sugar, celery salt, celery seed, salt, vinegar and salad oil. Bring to a full boil stirring frequently.
- Pour dressing over slaw.
- Refrigerate at least 4 hours.
- Before serving, toss to mix well.

Serves 6 to 8

"The home health aides were very wonderful caregivers and were always cheerful. My dad loved them and looked forward to seeing them."

Green Wonder Salad

Salad

1   (16 ounce) can sliced water chestnuts
1   (16 ounce) can white shoepeg corn
1   (16 ounce) can sliced carrots
1   (16 ounce) can French cut green beans
1   (16 ounce) can tiny green peas
1   (16 ounce) can bean sprouts
1   (2 ounce) jar pimento, diced
1½ cups celery, sliced thin
1   medium green pepper, sliced thin
2   red onions, sliced into thin rings
     Dressing (recipe follows)

• Drain all cans of vegetables. Mix water chestnuts, corn, carrots, green beans, peas, bean sprouts, pimento, celery, green pepper and red onions.

Dressing

1½ cups sugar
½   cup vegetable oil
½   cup water
1   cup vinegar
3-4 drops Tabasco sauce

• Combine sugar, oil, water, vinegar and Tabasco. Bring to a full boil.
• Pour dressing over vegetables and stir thoroughly.
• Let stand in refrigerator at least 24 hours before serving.
• Stir right before serving.

Serves 10 to 14

Southern Salad

1   (10 ounce) package frozen black-eyed peas
1   cup celery, sliced thin
1   cup diced tomatoes, drained
4-5 tablespoons French dressing
    Watercress
    Sweet onion rings, sliced thin

- Cook peas according to package directions. Drain and cool.
- Add celery, tomatoes and French dressing.
- Toss lightly and serve on bed of watercress.
- Garnish with onion rings.

Serves 4

Calico Bean Salad

2   tablespoons olive oil
2   tablespoons lime juice, freshly squeezed
2   tablespoons parsley, finely minced
1   teaspoon ground cumin
    Salt and pepper to taste
1¼ cups shoepeg corn, cooked and well drained
1   cup black beans, cooked and well drained
1   red bell pepper, diced
1   green pepper, diced
2   green onions, finely diced

- In a large bowl, whisk together oil, lime juice, parsley, cumin, salt and pepper.
- Add corn, beans, red and green peppers and green onions.
- Mix thoroughly.

Serves 8

The hamlet named Ninety Six was a vital political and economic center in the South Carolina back-country. Lt. Col. John Cruger took command and built the star fort. It was the heart of British defenses at Ninety Six and the stone upon which Gen. Nathanael Greene's well-planned siege stumbled. The fort survived and in 1974 archeologists found evidence of the patriots' siege trenches and restored the old outlines, including the original contours. There are few better examples of 18th-century siegecraft or of the close personal nature of battle in that day.

Club Chicken Salad

Salad
1   pound skinned and boned chicken breasts, cooked
3   small tomatoes, seeded and cut into strips
4   cups shredded iceberg lettuce
4   cups shredded leaf lettuce
2   strips bacon, cooked and crumbled
   Hot Bacon Dressing (recipe follows)

- While chicken is still warm, cut into strips and place in bowl with ½ cup hot bacon dressing. Set aside to cool to room temperature. In large bowl, toss tomatoes with both lettuces. Divide among 4 large salad plates.
- Arrange chicken on top and sprinkle with bacon. Drizzle 2 tablespoons dressing over top of each salad.

Serves 4

Hot Bacon Dressing
5   slices bacon, diced
½   cup finely chopped onion
   Vegetable oil
2   teaspoons corn starch
2   teaspoons water
½   cup white vinegar
½   cup water
¼   cup sugar
   Salt and pepper to taste

- Fry bacon until crisp. Drain on paper towels. Set aside.
- Add onion to bacon fat in skillet and cook about 5 minutes until onion is soft.
- With slotted spoon, add onion to bacon on paper towel.
- Pour bacon fat into measuring cup and add vegetable oil to equal ½ cup.
- Mix corn starch and water together. Add to bacon fat and set aside.

Club Chicken Salad *continued*

- Combine vinegar, water, sugar, salt and pepper in a small saucepan and heat to a boil. Add corn starch mixture and cook until thickened (1 to 2 minutes).
- Remove from heat and add bacon and onions. Use while warm.

1½ cups

Summer Rice Salad

This can make an excellent summer lunch or supper.

1	(6½ ounce) jar marinated artichoke hearts
⅓	cup mayonnaise
1	box chicken Rice-a-Roni
¼	teaspoon curry powder
½	cup green bell pepper, diced
6	green onions sliced (include green part)

- Remove artichokes from jar; add mayonnaise to remaining marinade in jar.
- Cook Rice-a-Roni as directed.
- Mix curry powder, bell pepper and green onions with rice mixture.
- Mix with mayonnaise and artichokes, stirring well.

Serves 6 to 8

To make a complete meal platter, serve surrounded with hard-cooked egg quarters, sliced tomatoes and asparagus spears rolled in boiled ham slices. This salad doesn't double well.

Cooking With Care 89

Located in the Northwest Greenwood County is historic Cokesbury College which was built in 1854 and was originally the Masonic Female Institute which was a female preparatory school. The building, which is listed on the National Register of Historic Places, served the youth of Cokesbury for 100 years. Today, the college building charms the traveler, entices the historian, and provides a unique setting for social occasions. The three-story brick building with stucco exterior is in the Greek Revival style and features an imposing double staircase leading to the second floor chapel. The chapel on the second floor can be reached by the exterior double staircase. In

Alaskan Fruit Salad

Children love this and can even help make it.

1   **envelope unflavored gelatin**
1½ **cups lemonade, divided**
1   **(3¼ ounce) package regular vanilla pudding mix**
½   **cup whipping cream**
1   **(11 ounce) can Mandarin orange sections, drained**
1   **(8¼ ounce) crushed pineapple, drained**
½   **cup maraschino cherries, quartered**

- Soften gelatin in ¼ cup of lemonade.
- In medium saucepan, combine 1¼ cups lemonade, pudding mix and softened gelatin. Cook and stir over medium heat until mixture thickens and bubbles.
- Chill until partially set.
- Whip cream; fold into gelatin mixture.
- Fold in oranges, pineapple and cherries.
- Chill until mixture mounds; turn into 4-cup mold.
- Chill 4 to 5 hours or overnight.
- Unmold and garnish with additional fruit, if desired.

Serves 6 to 8

Pretzel Strawberry Summer Salad

2	**cups plain pretzels, crushed**
½	**cup melted margarine or butter**
1	**tablespoon sugar**
1	**(8 ounce) package cream cheese, softened**
1	**cup sugar**
12	**ounces whipped topping**
1	**(6 ounce) package strawberry gelatin**
2	**cups boiling water**
20	**ounces frozen strawberries**

addition to its use as a chapel, this room also served as an auditorium for commencements and other public gatherings. The pews and other furnishings were donated from various churches.

- Preheat oven to 350°.
- Mix pretzels, margarine and 1 tablespoon sugar. Spread in 9 x 13 inch pan.
- Bake for 10 minutes. Let cool.
- Whip cream cheese, sugar, and whipped topping, mixing well.
- Spread over pretzel layer. Refrigerate.
- Mix gelatin, water and strawberries. Refrigerate until just thickened.
- Pour over cream cheese mixture.
- Refrigerate 2 to 4 hours.

Serves 10 to 12

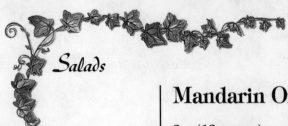

Mandarin Orange Salad

2 **(12 ounce) cans apricot nectar**
2 **(2.75 ounce) packages orange gelatin**
1 **(6 ounce) can frozen orange juice concentrate**
1 **(8 ounce) can crushed pineapple**
1 **(6 ounce) can Mandarin oranges, drained**

- Heat nectar to boiling. Add gelatin and stir until dissolved.
- Add orange juice, pineapple and oranges. Stir until thoroughly mixed.
- Pour into mold and refrigerate until thoroughly jelled.
- Unmold onto lettuce-lined platter.

Serves 6 to 8

Cloud Nine Cherry Salad

1 **(8 ounce) can crushed pineapple, drained**
1 **cup maraschino cherries, drained and chopped**
1 **(8 ounce) package cream cheese, softened**
1 **cup chopped nuts**
1 **(8 ounce) container frozen whipped topping, thawed**

- Combine pineapple, cherries and cream cheese; mix well.
- Add nuts and mix well.
- Fold in whipped topping.
- Serve in compote dish.

Serves 8 to 10

Basil Pecan Parmesan Salad Dressing

4	ounces olive oil
2	ounces balsamic vinegar
2	ounces pecans
2	ounces fresh basil
1	clove garlic, minced
1	ounce Parmesan cheese, grated
	Salt and coarse ground pepper to taste

- Puree olive oil, vinegar, pecans, basil, garlic and Parmesan cheese until smooth.
- Add salt and pepper.

1 cup

"The home health aides were so gentle and mother really enjoyed her baths. We love all of you."

Lemon Dill Salad Dressing

4	ounces olive oil
2	ounces lemon juice
1	bunch fresh dill, chopped
	Salt and coarse, ground pepper to taste

- Mix together olive oil, lemon juice and dill.
- Add salt and pepper.

1 cup

Sour Cream

1	cup mayonnaise
½	cup buttermilk
1	small onion, grated fine
	Garlic salt to taste
	Pinch of sugar

- Mix mayonnaise, buttermilk, onion, garlic salt and sugar until well blended. Serve on baked potatoes.

1½ cups

Clemson University Bleu Cheese was cured in Stumphouse Mountain Tunnel in 1941. Stumphouse originated from the Indian Legend of Isaqueena who fell in love with a silversmith who lived near Ninety Six, SC. Learning that her tribe planned a surprise attack on her lover's settlement, she mounted her pony and hastened to warn the settlers. On that fleet ride through the forest, she named the landmarks she passed en route: Mile Creek, Six Mile, Twelve Mile, Eighteen Mile, Three and Twenty, Six and Twenty and finally Ninety Six. It is actually 92 miles from her starting point to Ninety Six, SC.

Pioneers of southern industry dreamed of a railroad connecting the midwest with the busy port of Charleston, SC. The tunnel through Stumphouse Mountain was to be a vital link. The Civil War halted work; the tunnel was abandoned. Clemson

World's Best Bleu Cheese Dressing/Dip

3   pints sour cream
1½ pints mayonnaise
30 ounces Clemson Bleu Cheese Krumbles (or any kind of bleu cheese, crumbled)
1   tablespoon Worcestershire sauce
1½ teaspoons garlic salt
3   cups cultured buttermilk

- Combine sour cream, mayonnaise, bleu cheese, Worcestershire sauce, garlic salt, and buttermilk in large mixing bowl. Mix well.
- For dressing, add buttermilk to desired thickness.

7 pounds

Buttermilk Dressing

1   quart mayonnaise
3   cups buttermilk
1   teaspoon salt
1   teaspoon coarsely ground black pepper
1   teaspoon Accent
1   teaspoon garlic powder
1   teaspoon onion powder

- Mix mayonnaise, buttermilk, salt, pepper, Accent, garlic powder and onion powder well, but do not beat. Use as dip, salad dressing or on baked potato.

1¾ quarts

Keeps in refrigerator for weeks.

Blue Cheese Sour Cream Dressing

¼ **cup cream**
1 **cup sour cream**
¾ **blue cheese, crumbled**
¼ **teaspoon salt**
2 **tablespoons chili sauce**
¼ **clove garlic, minced**

- Blend cream, sour cream and blue cheese together.
- Add salt, chili sauce and garlic and mix well.
- Pour into jar; cover tightly and refrigerate until ready to serve.

1½ cups

Zestful Blue Cheese Dressing

½ **cup blue cheese, crumbled**
2 **tablespoons cider vinegar or lemon juice**
1 **cup mayonnaise**
½ **clove garlic, minced**
¼ **cup sour cream**
1 **tablespoon sugar**
   Dash salt

- Combine cheese, vinegar or lemon juice, mayonnaise, garlic, sour cream, sugar and salt.
- Beat until mixture is fluffy. Store in tightly covered container in refrigerator.

1½ cups

Variation: Add 3 tablespoons chopped pimiento.

College bought the tunnel in 1951. The tunnel measures 25' high by 17' wide and extends 1600' into the mountain. At the midway point, an air shaft extends upward 200' to the surface. Cold air moving out of the mouth of the tunnel pulls warm air down the shaft. The moisture in this warm air is condensed by the cold air to produce a constant wetness in the tunnel; favorable for curing blue cheese. An alert professor recognized the possibilities of curing blue mold cheese in the tunnel. Clemson Blue Cheese has always been an artisanal cheese, made the old fashioned way. Each 288 gallon vat makes a batch of about 240 pounds, which is then salted, waxed and aged for 6 months. When ready, each hoop is scraped and packaged by hand. Each lot is kept separate, and strenuous record keeping assures quality at every step.

Apple Dip

1   (8 ounce) package cream cheese, softened
⅓   cup firmly packed brown sugar
¼   cup sugar
1   teaspoon vanilla extract
1   (6 ounce) package almond brickle chips or English Toffee bits
      (available in the baking section of supermarket)
      Apple wedges (preferably Granny Smith)

- Combine cream cheese and brown sugar; mix well. Let stand 15 minutes.
- Stir in sugar, vanilla and brickle chips. Cover and chill at least 8 hours.
- Stir well before serving.

2½ cups

Fresh Fruit Dip

Good even without the fruit!

½   cup sugar
½   teaspoon salt
      Juice and zest of 1 orange
2   eggs, beaten
4   teaspoons cornstarch
      Juice and zest of 1 lemon
1   cup pineapple juice
1   (8 ounce) package cream cheese at room temperature

- Combine sugar, salt, orange juice, zest, eggs, cornstarch, lemon juice, zest and pineapple juice in the top of double boiler. Stir and cook until thick. Cool.
- Whip cream cheese until fluffy and mix thoroughly with other ingredients. Chill.
- Use as dip for fresh pineapple, strawberries or melon balls.

2½ cups

 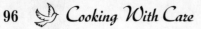

Entrées

Entrées

Chicken Pie Party Salad

This is the best chicken salad I've ever had. Great for summer luncheon and so different!

1   (9 ounce) frozen pie shell
1   (3 to 3½ pound) chicken (or 5 medium chicken breasts)
4   cups water
1½ teaspoons salt, divided
1   (9 ounce) can pineapple slices, diced
1   (3 ounce) can English walnuts (may use pecans if desired), chopped
½   cup diced celery
1   cup sour cream
⅔   cup mayonnaise
½   teaspoon salt
2   teaspoons lemon juice
1   tablespoon pineapple juice
     Sharp Cheddar cheese, finely shredded
     Parsley for color

- Bake pie shell according to directions on the package.
- Bring chicken, water and 1 teaspoon salt to boil in pan with tight fitting lid.
- Reduce heat and simmer until tender. Cool in broth to keep chicken from drying out.
- When cooled, remove meat from bones, skin and cut into bite size pieces.
- Drain pineapple, reserving 1 tablespoon juice.
- Combine chicken, pineapple, walnuts and celery.
- In a separate bowl, combine the sour cream, mayonnaise, ½ teaspoon salt, lemon juice and pineapple juice.
- Add about ⅓ of the sauce to the chicken mixture. Refrigerate both mixtures overnight.
- Just before serving, fill baked pie shell with the chicken salad, and ice the pie with the remaining sauce.
- Sprinkle with finely shredded cheese and decorate with a sprig of parsley for each slice of pie.

Serves 5 per pie, plus some chicken leftover

Why not double the recipe to make 3 pies and have a luncheon?

Chicken Chili Lasagna

This is a must try!

2   (3 ounce) packages cream cheese
1   medium onion, chopped
2   bunches green onions, chopped
8   ounces finely shredded Mexican cheese, divided
2   garlic cloves, minced
¾   teaspoon ground cumin, divided
½   teaspoon minced fresh cilantro or parsley
3   cups cubed cooked chicken or turkey
¼   cup margarine
¼   cup all-purpose flour
1-1½ cups chicken broth
4   ounces shredded Monterey Jack cheese
1   cup sour cream
1   (4 ounce) can chopped green chiles, drained
⅛   teaspoon dried thyme
    Salt and pepper to taste
12 (6 inch) flour tortillas, halved

- Preheat oven to 350°.
- In mixing bowl, combine cream cheese, onions, 1½ cups Mexican cheese blend, garlic, ¼ teaspoon cumin and cilantro.
- Stir in chicken; set aside.
- In a saucepan, melt margarine. Stir in flour until smooth; gradually add broth. Bring to a boil; cook and stir for 2 minutes or until thickened.
- Remove from heat. Stir in Monterey Jack cheese, sour cream, chiles, thyme, salt, pepper and remaining cumin.
- Spread ½ cup of the cheese sauce in a greased 13 x 9 inch baking dish.
- Top with 6 tortilla halves, a third of the chicken mixture and ¼ of the cheese sauce.
- Repeat tortilla, chicken and cheese sauce layers twice.
- Top with remaining tortillas, cheese sauce and Mexican cheese.

Chicken Chili Lasagna *continued*

- Cover and bake for 30 minutes.
- Uncover; bake 10 minutes longer or until heated through.
- Let stand 5 minutes before cutting.

Serves 12

Savory Chicken Squares

3 ounces cream cheese
2 tablespoons margarine
2 cups cooked diced chicken or turkey
¼ teaspoon salt
⅛ teaspoon pepper
2 tablespoons milk
1 tablespoon chopped onion
1 tablespoon pimento, chopped
1 (8 ounce) can crescent rolls
   Melted butter
   Italian bread crumbs
1 (10¾ ounce) can cream of chicken soup

- Preheat oven to 350°.
- Blend cream cheese and margarine.
- Mix chicken, salt, pepper, milk, onion and pimento together.
- Separate crescent rolls. Form into rectangular shape by sealing the two rolls together. Roll dough a little to make thinner.
- Spoon ½ cup of chicken mixture in center of dough. Bring 4 corners together and pinch together to seal.
- Brush top with melted butter and sprinkle with bread crumbs.
- Bake on greased baking sheet for 20 to 25 minutes.
- Serve with cream sauce made with soup diluted with milk. Use only enough to make a cream sauce.

Serves 4 to 6

Crock Pot Style Turkey Breast

1 turkey breast
Apple juice

- Place a wire rack inside the crock pot.
- Pour enough apple juice into the pot to touch the rack.
- Bring juice to a boil and place the crock pot on the pre-heated base.
- Place a washed turkey breast on the rack.
- Cover and cook approximately 6 to 7 hours on low.
- Let stand 30 minutes. This makes the turkey very moist and flavorful.

Serves 6 to 8 (depending on size of turkey breast)

"...thank you again for the wonderful attention I've gotten from your organization since I was introduced to hospice. The night my husband died, a wonderful nurse came and took care of everything. I don't remember when she left - so I possibly didn't even thank her. But I have thanked God many times since that night for sending her to us. Thank you from the bottom of my heart."

Baked Chicken Breasts

8 chicken breast halves, skinned and boned
8 (¼ inch) slices Swiss cheese
1 (4 ounce) jar sliced mushrooms
1 (10¾ ounce) can cream of chicken soup, undiluted
½ cup dry white wine
1 cup herb seasoned stuffing mix, crushed
¼ cup butter or margarine, melted

- Preheat oven to 350°.
- Arrange chicken in a lightly greased 13 x 9 inch baking dish.
- Top with cheese slices.
- Sauté mushrooms in a small amount of butter or margarine.
- Combine soup and wine; stir well. Add mushrooms.
- Spoon evenly over chicken; sprinkle with stuffing mix.
- Drizzle butter over stuffing mix.
- Bake 45 to 55 minutes.

Serves 8

Hawaiian Chicken Salad

2   **cups cooked chicken, cubed**
1   **cup chopped celery**
1   **cup mayonnaise**
½   **teaspoon nutmeg**
1   **(20 ounce) can chunk pineapple, drained.**
1   **(11 ounce) can Mandarin oranges, drained**
½   **cup flaked coconut**
¾   **cup peanuts or salted cashews**
2   **large firm bananas, sliced**

- Toss chicken, celery, mayonnaise, and nutmeg mixing well.
- Cover and chill for at least 30 minutes.
- Before serving, add fruits and coconut.
- Sprinkle with nuts and serve on leafy salad greens.

Serves 6

Italian Chicken and Rice

1   **(12 ounce) boneless chicken breast, cut into strips**
½   **cup chopped onion**
1   **cup chicken broth**
1   **(14½ ounce) can diced tomatoes with garlic, basil and oregano - do not drain**
1½ **cups instant white rice**
1   **(14½ ounce) can French style green beans, drained**

- Coat a large skillet with nonstick cooking spray, and heat on medium to high heat.
- Add chicken strips and onion.
- Cook and stir 3 minutes or until chicken is no longer pink.
- Stir in broth and tomatoes.
- Bring to a boil, and stir in rice and beans.
- Reduce heat, and simmer covered for 5 minutes.
- Remove from heat and serve with grated Parmesan cheese, if desired.

Serves 4

Chicken Spectacular

4   cups cooked chicken, pulled apart
1   (6 ounce) box wild rice, cooked per instructions on the box
1   cup mayonnaise
1   (10¾ ounce) can cream of celery soup
1   medium onion, chopped
1   (2 ounce) jar pimento
1   (4 ounce) can water chestnuts, chopped
1   roll of Ritz crackers, crushed
1½ sticks margarine, melted

- Preheat oven to 350°.
- Mix together chicken, cooked rice, mayonnaise, soup, onion, pimento, and water chestnuts.
- Put mixture in 9 x 13 inch pan.
- Sprinkle crushed crackers on top.
- Pour melted margarine over the crackers.
- Bake for 30 to 45 minutes.

Serves 8 to 10

Curried Chicken Casserole

4	chicken breasts cut into 1 inch strips
2	tablespoons olive oil
1	(10¾ ounce) can cream of chicken soup
½	cup mayonnaise
1	tablespoon curry powder (or to taste)
	Salt and pepper to taste
1	can asparagus, drained (or may use fresh) or substitute broccoli
1	cup shredded Cheddar cheese

- Preheat oven to 350°.
- Cook chicken strips in olive oil until done.
- Mix soup, mayonnaise, curry powder, salt and pepper.
- Place asparagus on the bottom of an 8 or 9 inch casserole dish.
- Cover the asparagus with the chicken strips and then the soup mixture.
- Sprinkle the cheese on top.
- Bake for 30 minutes.

Serves 4

Cheesy Chicken Roll-Ups

1   (10¾ ounce) cream of chicken soup
1   cup milk
¾   cup shredded Cheddar cheese, divided
1   package crescent rolls
1½ cups cooked chicken, cubed

- Preheat oven to 350°.
- In saucepan, combine soup, milk and half of the cheese.
- Heat until cheese melts.
- Pour half of this mixture into an ungreased 8 or 9 inch baking dish. Save rest for gravy.
- Combine chicken with ¼ cup cheese.
- Separate dinner roll triangles. Place chicken mixture on triangles and roll.
- Place rolls in the dish and sprinkle remaining cheese on top.
- Bake for 25 to 35 minutes or until rolls are browned.

Serves 4

Chicken Wendall

2   **cups salad shrimp, cooked**
6-8 **sun-dried tomatoes, finely chopped**
1   **tablespoon basil pesto**
1   **medium red pepper, finely chopped**
1   **medium green bell pepper, finely chopped**
1   **small red onion, finely chopped**
¾   **cup bread crumbs, divided**
2   **eggs**
6   **(6 ounce) chicken breasts (skinless, boneless)**
     Butter
6   **ounces Boursin cheese**

- Preheat oven to 375°.
- Combine shrimp, tomatoes, pesto, peppers, onion, bread crumbs and eggs and stir well.
- Pound chicken breasts to even thickness; place about ½ cup of mixture to one side; fold and secure with a toothpick.
- Melt butter and sauté stuffed breast on both sides just until brown.
- Top with a tablespoon of Boursin cheese, sprinkle with bread crumbs and bake for approximately 12 to 15 minutes.

Serves 6

"We love you and God bless each and every one of you."

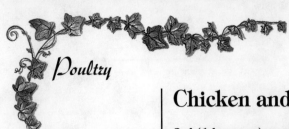

Chicken and Artichoke Casserole

3-4 (14 ounce) cans water-packed artichokes
4   tablespoons olive oil
3   cloves garlic, minced
3   cups cooked, cubed chicken
2   (10¾ ounce) cans cream of chicken soup
1   cup mayonnaise
2   teaspoons lemon juice
½   teaspoon curry powder
1¼ cups shredded Cheddar cheese (5 ounces)
¾   cup Romano cheese
¾   cup bread crumbs
2   tablespoons butter

- Preheat oven to 350°.
- Drain artichoke hearts and quarter.
- Mix olive oil and garlic in bowl. Add artichoke hearts and toss.
- Spread in 9 x 13 inch baking dish.
- Arrange cubed chicken over artichokes.
- In medium bowl, mix together soup, mayonnaise, lemon juice and curry powder and pour over chicken.
- Top with Cheddar cheese and Romano cheese.
  (Can be refrigerated overnight at this point).
- Toss bread crumbs with melted butter and spread on top of cheese.
- Bake for 25 minutes or slightly longer if dish has been refrigerated.

Serves 8 to 12

Country Captains

½ cup all-purpose flour
1   teaspoon salt
½ teaspoon white pepper
6   chicken breast halves (with or without skin)
    Vegetable oil
4   small onions, diced
2   medium green bell peppers, chopped
1   clove garlic, minced
2   (16 ounce) cans tomatoes, undrained and chopped
¼ cup currants
1-2 teaspoons curry powder
    Salt and white pepper to taste
½ teaspoon thyme
3   cups cooked rice
½ cup slivered almonds, toasted

- Preheat oven to 350°.
- Combine flour, salt and pepper. Dredge chicken in flour mixture.
- Fry chicken in ½ inch hot oil until browned; drain well and arrange chicken in a 13 x 9 inch baking dish.
- Reserve 2 tablespoons drippings from skillet.
- Sauté onions, peppers and garlic in reserved drippings until tender.
- Add tomatoes, currants, curry powder, salt, white pepper and thyme; stir well, and spoon over chicken.
- Cover and bake for 55 minutes to 1 hour or until done.
- Remove chicken to large serving platter and spoon rice around chicken.
- Spoon vegetables and sauce over rice and sprinkle with almonds.

Serves 6

"Our social worker was great. She always saw that I got what I needed and was so nice."

Fried chicken is arguably the quintessential Southern dish. Barbecue may well be the only other Southern specialty with more fierce pride behind it. Another popular method of deep- frying poultry in the South involves frying the whole bird, such as a turkey. It makes for a very crisp skin and moist meat.

To fry a whole turkey, you need a 10 gallon pot and around 5 gallons of oil. Frying turkey must be done outdoors. Once you've eaten fried turkey, you'll never go back to baked. It isn't greasy as one tends to think it might be. Coat the entire turkey with a rub for poultry. Fry the turkey for about 3 to 4 minutes per pound or until it is evenly golden brown all over and the meat thermometer reads 180°.

Southern Fried Chicken and Gravy

Fried Chicken

1   **(3 pound) broiler-fryer, cut up**
    Salt and pepper to taste
2   **cups all-purpose flour**
1   **teaspoon red pepper**
1   **egg, slightly beaten**
½   **cup milk**
    Vegetable oil
    Gravy (recipe follows)

- Sprinkle chicken pieces with salt and pepper.
- Combine flour and red pepper; set aside.
- Combine egg and milk; whisk well.
- Dip chicken in egg mixture and dredge in flour, coating well.
- Heat 1 inch of oil in a heavy skillet, place chicken in skillet. Cover chicken and cook over medium heat 20 to 25 minutes or until golden brown; turn occasionally.
- Drain on paper towels before serving.

Serves 4 to 6

Gravy

¼   **cup pan drippings**
¼   **cup all-purpose flour**
2½ **cups hot milk**
    Salt and pepper to taste

- Pour off all except ¼ cup drippings from skillet in which chicken was fried; place skillet over medium heat. Add flour and stir vigorously until browned.
- Gradually add hot milk stirring constantly.
- Cook and stir until thickened.
- Add salt and pepper.

2¾ cups

Apricot Pecan Chicken

4   **chicken breast halves (with or without skin)**
½   **cup apricot preserves**
2   **tablespoons cider vinegar**
1   **clove garlic, minced**
1   **tablespoon soy sauce**
1   **teaspoon ground ginger**
½   **cup pecans, chopped**
     Fresh black pepper

- Preheat oven to 350°.
- Place chicken breasts in a 9 x 13 inch pan.
- Mix together apricot preserves, vinegar, garlic, soy sauce, ginger, pecans and pepper.
- Baste chicken with apricot mixture and bake for about 30 minutes or until done. Baste every 10 minutes during cooking time.
- Last 5 minutes of cooking, turn oven to broil. Lightly brown chicken before serving.

Serves 2 to 4

Saluda County

Celebrating 100 years of existence as a county, Saluda is proud of her heritage. In 1895, in an ordinance of the Constitutional Convention, a portion of Edgefield County was separated to form Saluda County. "Saluda" means *river of corn* in the language of the Cherokee Indians whose homes and hunting grounds were up and down the Saluda River. From Saluda two young men lived and made their way across a young, restless country eventually to meet again at an abandoned Spanish Mission in South Texas called the Alamo. Those two friends, William Barrett Travis and James Butler Bonham, grew up in Saluda County. Here they acquired a sense of loyalty, duty and honor that would sustain them as they held on to their dream of Texas, and held off Santa Anna and the Mexican Army for

Parmesan Chicken

1	cup grated Parmesan cheese
2	cups soft bread crumbs
⅓	cup melted margarine
½	cup honey mustard salad dressing
6	chicken breasts, skinned and deboned

- Preheat oven to 425°.
- Combine cheese, bread crumbs and margarine.
- Coat chicken with honey mustard then dip in bread crumb mixture.
- Place breaded chicken in a greased 13 x 9 inch baking pan.
- Bake for 15 to 20 minutes (uncovered) or until chicken is done.

Serves 4 to 6

Ann's Chicken Divan

2½	cups cooked chicken, diced
1	(10 ounce) package frozen broccoli
¼	cup light cream
1	(10¾ ounce) can cream of chicken soup
1	tablespoon cooking sherry
⅛	teaspoon nutmeg
½	cup Cheddar cheese, shredded

- Preheat oven to 450°.
- Place the chicken in a greased 11 x 7 inch baking dish and top with broccoli.
- In a small bowl, mix cream, soup, sherry and nutmeg.
- Pour over chicken and broccoli.
- Sprinkle cheese on top and bake uncovered 15 to 20 minutes.

Serves 4

Chicken Marbella

8   chicken breasts, skin removed, bone in
1   cup balsamic vinegar
½   cup virgin olive oil
1½ tablespoons dried oregano
1½ tablespoons dried basil
16 ounces green olives (stuffed with pimentos, garlic
      or jalapeño), drained
16 ounces moist prunes
4   ounces capers packed in brine, drained
1   cup dry white wine
½   cup dark brown sugar
½   cup Italian parsley (flat)

- Preheat oven to 350°.
- Place breasts in non-reactive bowl with tight lid.
- Make marinade by mixing vinegar, oil, oregano and basil (can also be blended to make a thicker marinade). Pour over breasts.
- Add olives, prunes and capers.
- Marinate 24 to 48 hours in refrigerator; turn or shake bowl every 6 to 8 hours to coat all pieces well.
- Place breasts in single layer in non-reactive pan, bone down.
- Pour remaining marinade over meat.
- Add wine to pan; sprinkle with brown sugar.
- Place pan in oven and bake for 50 to 60 minutes or until juices run clear and breasts are dark golden brown.
- Sprinkle with parsley and serve with wild rice or mashed potatoes. Serve with pan juices.

Serves 8

13 days. Both of these heroes are honored on the grounds of the courthouse.

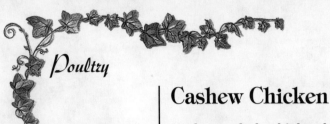

Cashew Chicken

2   large whole chicken breasts, skinned, deboned
¼   cup water
¼   cup dry sherry
¼   cup soy sauce
1   tablespoon plus 1 teaspoon cornstarch
2   tablespoons dark corn syrup
1   tablespoon vinegar
¼   cup peanut oil
½   cup chopped green pepper
1   (4 ounce) can water chestnuts, drained and sliced
½   cup cashews
2   tablespoons sliced green onions
2   cloves garlic, minced
¼   teaspoon ground ginger
1   (10 ounce) package frozen pea pods or sugar peas
2-3 cups cooked rice

- Cut chicken into 1 inch pieces; set aside.
- Combine water, sherry, soy sauce, cornstarch, corn syrup and vinegar; mix well and set aside.
- Heat wok to 375° or high heat for 2 minutes. Coat sides of wok with oil.
- Add chicken; stir fry 2 to 3 minutes or until chicken turns white, push up sides of wok.
- Add green pepper, water chestnuts and cashews; stir fry 30 seconds, push up sides of wok.
- Add onion, garlic and ginger; stir fry 1 minute; push up sides.
- Add pea pods, stir fry 30 seconds.
- Add cornstarch mixture, bring to a boil, stirring constantly, cook an additional minute stirring all ingredients with sauce.
- Serve over hot cooked rice.

Serves 4

Black Raspberry Glazed Chicken Breasts with Wild Rice Stuffing

1   (7 ounce) package wild and long grain rice mix
2   cups chicken broth
½   cup slivered almonds, toasted
½   cup seedless black raspberry jam (other jam flavors work also)
2   tablespoons frozen orange juice concentrate
½   cup honey
1   teaspoon orange zest
8   boneless, skinless chicken breasts, slightly flattened
    Salt, paprika and garlic powder to taste
1   cup all-purpose flour
½   cup butter

- Preheat oven to 325°.
- Prepare rice mix substituting broth for water. Toss rice with almonds. Set aside.
- In a small saucepan, heat jam, orange juice concentrate, honey and zest until blended and heated through. Set aside.
- Sprinkle chicken with salt, paprika and garlic powder. Place about ¼ cup rice on flattened chicken; roll and secure with toothpicks.
- Dredge chicken in flour.
- Melt butter in 9 x 13 inch baking dish; coat each chicken roll with butter. Layer in dish; bake 40 minutes.
- Baste with raspberry glaze and continue baking and basting until tender (about an additional 30 minutes). May be served with additional rice.

Serves 8

"We especially want to thank the volunteers. You all are a great group of people. Words cannot express our gratitude and appreciation."

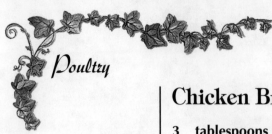

Pascal's, a bistro-style restaurant, is owned and operated by Lisa and Pascal Hurtibize. It is located in midtown Greenwood in a lovely house, giving it just the right ambiance for the wonderful food that is served. The food, prepared by Pascal, is always delicious and there is a nice variety; gourmet, as well as steaks and seafood. It is served with an excellent variety of wines.

Chicken Breasts with Artichokes

3   tablespoons butter, divided
8   skinless, boneless chicken breast halves
4   ounces dry white wine
1   large sweet onion, cut in half and then into slices
1   (9 ounce) package frozen artichoke hearts, thawed and cut
     into halves
6   ounces chicken stock
1   teaspoon dried thyme
     Salt and freshly ground pepper to taste
1   lemon, thinly sliced

• In a 4 quart heavy-bottomed pot over medium to medium-high heat, melt 2 tablespoons of the butter. Working in batches, if necessary, add the chicken breasts and brown on all sides until they are a rich gold, 8 to 10 minutes; do not allow the butter to become dark brown.

• Using a slotted spoon, transfer the breasts to a 9 x 13 inch baking dish.

• Pour the wine into the pot and, using a large spoon, deglaze over medium-high heat by stirring to dislodge any browned bits from the pot bottom.

• Pour the liquid over the chicken. Wipe pot clean.

• In the same pot over medium heat, melt the remaining 1 tablespoon butter. Add the onion and sauté, stirring, until translucent, about 5 minutes.

• Return the chicken and juices to the pot and add the artichokes, chicken stock and thyme.

• Stir well and bring to a simmer over medium-low heat. Cover and simmer gently until the chicken is tender and cooked through, 20 to 25 minutes. (To test, cut into a chicken breast with sharp knife; the meat should be opaque throughout.)

• Season to taste with salt and pepper.

• Spoon into warmed shallow bowls, and garnish with the lemon slices and serve.

Serves 8

Standing Rib Roast

1 **(7 pound) standing rib roast**
2 **tablespoons salt**
1 **tablespoon garlic powder**
1 **tablespoon onion powder**
1 **teaspoon ground thyme**
1 **teaspoon ground bay leaf (*lauris nobilis* - not California bay)**
1 **teaspoon fresh ground pepper**

- Preheat oven to 325°.
- Combine salt, garlic powder, onion powder, thyme, bay leaf and pepper. Sprinkle roast with spices.
- Place roast, fat side up, on rack in a shallow roasting pan. Insert meat thermometer, making sure it does not touch fat or bone.
- Bake roast as follows for the desired degree of doneness: rare, 20 minutes per pound (140°); medium, 25 minutes per pound (160°); well done, 35 minutes per pound or (170°).

Serves 12

Probably the most common cut, certainly the most recognizable, that comes from the rib is the standing rib roast. This is the king of beef roasts in the United States. In selecting a standing rib, ask for the small end. It may be a bit more expensive, but it is worth it. It should be trimmed so that the rib bones are no more than seven or eight inches in length, with the chine bone, feather bones and back strap removed. If not, carving will be a problem. Don't even bother with less than a three-rib roast, any less than that is not a roast but rather a thick steak and would be better treated as such.

Easy Beef Burgundy

2½ **pound round steak, cut into bite size pieces**
1 **(10¾ ounce) can Golden Mushroom soup**
1 **package onion soup mix**
1 **(6 ounce) jar sliced mushrooms, undrained**
½ **cup Burgundy**

- Combine meat, mushroom soup, onion soup, mushrooms and burgundy in a casserole dish with a tight fitting lid.
- Preheat oven to 250 to 300°.
- Bake for 3 hours without opening the oven door.
- Serve over rice or wide noodles.

Serves 4 to 6

Grilled London Broil

1½ **pounds flank steak**
1   **cup olive oil**
¼   **cup balsamic vinegar**
¼   **cup soy sauce**
4-6 **garlic cloves, minced**
½   **cup chopped fresh parsley**
¼   **cup chopped fresh basil**
½   **teaspoon ground black pepper**

- Score steak diagonally across the grain at ¾ inch intervals.
- Combine oil, vinegar, soy sauce, garlic, parsley, basil and pepper.
- Place steak and marinade in zip top bag or shallow covered dish. Marinate in refrigerator at least 8 hours.
- Remove steak from marinade. Reserve marinade and bring to a boil in a small saucepan.
- Grill steak 8 to 10 minutes on each side or until desired doneness.
- Baste steak with marinade the last 5 minutes.
- To serve, slice steak diagonally across the grain into thin slices.

Serves 4 to 6

Hungarian Goulash

1   tablespoon butter
2   pounds beef round or chuck cut in 1 inch cubes
    Salt and pepper to taste
2   medium green bell peppers, cut in 1 inch pieces
2   medium onions, diced
1¼ cups chicken broth
¼   cup dry white wine
3   tablespoons tomato paste or 1 (8 ounce) can tomato sauce
2-4 teaspoons Hungarian paprika (regular paprika will not do)
3   medium red potatoes, cut in 1½ inch pieces
1½ cups sour cream
½   cup caraway seeds (optional)

- Melt butter in large heavy frying pan or Dutch oven over medium heat.
- Brown beef on all sides.
- Season with salt and pepper.
- Add bell peppers, onions and broth.
- Stir together wine, tomato paste and paprika. Caution - add paprika a little at a time until it suits your taste or it might be too hot. Add to pan.
- Cover and simmer gently until meat is tender, about 1½ to 2 hours. May have to add a little more broth.
- Add potatoes and cook until just tender.
- Stir in sour cream and caraway seed.

Serves 8

World's Best Meatballs

Oil
½   **cup unseasoned bread crumbs**
⅓   **cup milk**
2   **eggs**
2   **pounds ground sirloin**
¼   **cup tomato sauce**
2   **teaspoons salt**
½   **teaspoon oregano**
½   **teaspoon dried basil**
¼   **teaspoon nutmeg**
¼   **teaspoon black pepper**
1   **(14.5 ounce) can beef broth**
1   **(14.5 ounce) can crushed tomatoes**
2   **tablespoons tomato paste**

- Preheat oven to 450°.
- Lightly oil 13 x 9 inch pan.
- Mix crumbs and milk in a large bowl. Let soften.
- Add eggs, meat, tomato sauce, salt, oregano, basil, nutmeg and pepper.
- Shape into meatballs using ¼ cup for each meatball.
- Place in pan and brush with oil. Bake for 20 minutes. Drain excess fat.
- Mix broth, tomatoes, tomato paste and add to pan.
- Cover and bake for 45 minutes.

Serves 8

Meatloaf Brocciolla

1   **pound ground chuck**
1   **(4 ounce) can sliced mushrooms, drained**
½   **cup bread crumbs**
1   **egg, slightly beaten**
¼   **teaspoon garlic powder**
    Salt and pepper to taste
½   **cup water**
3   **thin slices boiled ham**
4   **slices bacon, fried and crumbled**
1   **teaspoon parsley, chopped**
¼   **teaspoon oregano**
¼   **teaspoon basil**
¼   **teaspoon thyme**
1   **cup grated mozzarella cheese**
1   **medium onion, chopped**
1   **(16 ounce) can tomato sauce**

- Preheat oven to 350°.
- Mix ground chuck, mushrooms, bread crumbs, egg, garlic, salt, pepper and water thoroughly and refrigerate for about ½ hour.
- Roll out refrigerated meat mixture into oblong shape. Place ham slices evenly over mixture.
- Sprinkle with crumbled bacon, parsley, oregano, basil, thyme, cheese and onion.
- Roll snugly and place in loaf pan.
- Pour tomato sauce over meat.
- Bake for 50 to 60 minutes or until meat is done.

Serves 6 to 8

"You did so much - so many wonderful gestures of help and understanding-Thank you from all of our family, but especially from me. She was my precious wife."

Meatball Casserole

9-10   slices bacon
1   hamburger bun, stale
⅓   cup milk
2   eggs
2   tablespoons ketchup
1   tablespoon Worcestershire sauce
        Salt and pepper to taste
2   pounds ground beef
2   large onions, thinly sliced
1   (10¾ ounce) can cream of mushroom soup
1   (10¾ ounce) can beef consommé

- Preheat oven to 400°.
- In heavy skillet, cook bacon until crisp and set aside.
- In large bowl, crumble bun in milk until mushy. Add eggs, ketchup, Worcestershire sauce, salt, pepper and ground beef. Mix thoroughly.
- Form into small balls - about 1 inch in diameter - and brown quickly in skillet used for frying bacon. As meatballs brown, arrange a layer in a 9 x 13 inch casserole dish.
- Place a layer of onion over meatballs and continue layering meatballs and onions until all are used.
- Pour both cans of soup into skillet; heat to mix. Pour over meatballs.
- Crumble bacon on top.
- Bake for 1 hour (covered).

Serves 8 to 10

Sauerbraten with Potato Dumplings

Meat

3	pound boneless chuck or bottom round roast
3	quarts water
1	large onion
1½	cups white vinegar
3	cups sugar
1	jar pickling spices, tied in cheesecloth
1	box ginger snaps
	Water to make paste
	Potato Dumplings (recipe follows)

"Mother looked forward to her volunteers' visits. She loved them and valued their friendship. God Bless You All."

- Place meat, water, onion, vinegar, sugar and pickling spices in a large pot. Cover and simmer 8 hours.
- Make paste of ginger snaps and water, stir into meat mixture.
- Cover and simmer 1 hour, stirring occasionally.

Potato Dumplings

4-6	medium potatoes
	Salt and pepper to taste
	Butter to taste
2	cups flour, divided
1	egg, slightly beaten
	Several slices toasted bread, cut into cubes

- Boil potatoes in their jackets until tender, peel and mash with salt, pepper and butter.
- Stir in 1 cup flour and egg.
- Sprinkle extra flour on cutting board.
- Take about ¼ cup potato mixture, flatten and place 2 to 3 bread cubes in center.
- Form into ball, continue with remaining potatoes and bread cubes.
- Drop into boiling water and simmer 6 minutes.
- Serve hot with sauerbraten.

Serves 6 to 8

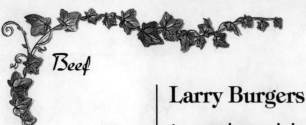

Larry Burgers

1	pound ground chuck
¼	teaspoon oregano
¼	teaspoon garlic powder
¼	teaspoon seasoned salt
1	egg, slightly beaten
⅛	cup steak sauce
⅛	cup honey

- Mix meat, oregano, garlic, salt, egg, steak sauce and honey thoroughly.
- Form into 4 patties and chill until ready to grill.
- Cook to desired doneness.

Serves 4

Taco Salad

This is a very popular lunch dish.

1	pound lean ground beef
1	package taco seasoning mix
1	(15 ounce) bag taco flavored Doritos
3	tomatoes or 1 package cherry tomatoes, diced
1	head iceberg lettuce, chopped
1	(4 ounce) can black olives, drained and sliced
2	cups taco flavored shredded Cheddar cheese
1	(16 ounce) bottle Catalina dressing

- In heavy skillet, cook meat until brown. Drain.
- Add seasoning mix and stir well.
- Crumble ½ bag of Doritos and mix with meat mixture. Chill well.
- Combine tomatoes, lettuce, black olives, cheese and dressing. Add meat mixture and mix well; place in large salad bowl.
- After salad is thoroughly mixed, decorate edges of salad bowl with remaining Doritos (don't crush).

Serves 6 to 8

Tom's Hash

8   **pounds lean beef, such as bottom round**
4   **pounds fresh pork**
12 **pounds onions, chopped**
2   **pounds potatoes, grated (optional)**
4   **tablespoons salt**
6   **teaspoons pepper**
⅔   **cup apple cider vinegar**
1½ **teaspoons crushed red pepper**
1   **stick butter**

- In a very large pot, cover meat with water and cook on low heat until meat can be torn into pieces.
- Remove meat from liquid, allow to cool and tear into pieces.
- Dip out half of the liquid and replace with water.
- Put meat back into water, along with the onions, and let simmer for several minutes on low heat.
- Add salt, pepper, vinegar, red pepper and butter.
- Cook until desired consistency, stirring frequently, about 2½ to 3 hours.
- If you choose to add potatoes (we do), add 15 to 20 minutes before finished, so that they will dissolve and absorb liquid in pot.

16 to 20 Quarts

Carolina Hash exists in two distinct varieties-the Lowcountry version is usually pork based. Some old fashioned recipes call for using the meat from a hogshead and sometimes organ meats such as pork liver. High-on-the-hog hash can be made with Boston Butt. Lowcountry hashers always include potatoes in their hash, while Upcountry hashers often use beef and exclude potatoes. Lowcountry hash is always served over rice; Upcountry hash is often served with bread or with grits. You can find many recipes for barbeque hash; every township in South Carolina thinks theirs is the only real hash. Try it, you'll like it.

Enchilada Casserole

2	pounds ground beef
1	medium onion, chopped
2	(8 ounce) cans tomato sauce
1	(11 ounce) can Mexicorn, drained
1	(10 ounce) can enchilada sauce
1	teaspoon chili powder
½	teaspoon dried oregano
½	teaspoon pepper
¼	teaspoon salt
1	(6½ ounce) package corn tortillas, divided
2	cups shredded Cheddar cheese, divided

- Preheat oven to 375°.
- Cook beef and onions in a large skillet until beef is browned, stirring until it crumbles; drain well.
- Stir tomato sauce, Mexicorn, enchilada sauce, chili powder, oregano, pepper and salt into meat mixture.
- Bring to a boil. Reduce heat to medium and cook uncovered 5 minutes, stirring occasionally.
- Place half of tortillas in bottom of a greased 13 x 9 inch baking dish.
- Spoon half of beef mixture over tortillas; sprinkle with 1 cup cheese.
- Repeat layers with remaining tortillas and beef mixture.
- Bake for 10 minutes.
- Sprinkle with remaining cheese and bake 5 more minutes or until cheese melts.

Serves 8

Honey Mustard Pork Chops

3   **tablespoons Dijon mustard**
3   **tablespoons light brown sugar**
¼   **cup honey**
6   **center cut thick pork chops**

- Combine mustard, brown sugar and honey.
- Place pork chops in shallow dish with lid and add marinade.
- Marinate in refrigerator at least 3 hours or overnight.
- Grill or broil until done.

Serves 4 to 6

Oriental Pork Tenderloin

½   **cup soy sauce**
½   **cup teriyaki sauce**
3   **tablespoons brown sugar**
2   **green onions, chopped**
2   **cloves garlic, chopped**
1   **tablespoon toasted sesame seeds**
½   **teaspoon ground ginger**
1   **tablespoon vegetable oil**
3   **pounds pork tenderloin (not loin)**

- Mix soy sauce, teriyaki sauce, brown sugar, green onions, garlic, sesame seeds, ginger and oil in a bowl.
- Add pork to coat. Marinate 6 to 8 hours, covered and refrigerated.
- Put pork in a 9 x 13 inch pan. Bake uncovered for 30 minutes to 1 hour (until meat thermometer reads 160°).
- Baste meat with marinade while baking.
- Slice meat thin and serve with drippings from the pan.

Serves 8

Tender Pork Kabobs

2   **pounds pork tenderloin (not boneless pork loin)**
¾   **cup firmly packed light brown sugar**
¾   **cup water**
¾   **cup French dressing**
¾   **cup Italian dressing**
⅓   **cup red wine vinegar**

- Cut meat in half crosswise. Cut each piece into 13 thin strips lengthwise.
- Combine sugar, water, dressings and vinegar in a small mixing bowl and pour into a plastic zip bag or shallow dish with lid, reserving ½ cup of marinade. Add meat. Refrigerate at least 8 hours.
- Remove meat from marinade and discard liquid. Thread strips onto 12 inch skewers.
- Grill over medium to high heat (350° to 400°) 5 to 8 minutes on each side, basting with reserved marinade.

26 Kabobs

Brunswick Stew

Freeze this hearty stew in several small containers.

1   (3 pound) broiler-fryer chicken
1½ pounds beef stew meat, cut into 1 inch pieces
1   pound pork tenderloin
3   (16 ounce) cans diced tomatoes, undrained
1   (6 ounce) can tomato paste
6   red potatoes, peeled and cubed
1   (16 ounce) package frozen white corn
3   medium jalapeño peppers, seeded and diced
4   cups frozen lima beans
4   cups chopped onion
2   cups sliced carrots
2   cups sliced okra
1   cup frozen green peas
1   cup chopped cabbage
1   tablespoon sugar
3   tablespoons Worcestershire sauce
2   tablespoons lemon juice
2   teaspoons salt
1   teaspoon pepper

According to one story, Brunswick stew was named for Brunswick County, Virginia, where in 1828 Dr. Creed Haskins of the Virginia state legislature asked for a special squirrel stew from "Uncle Jimmy" Matthews to feed people attending a political rally. The origin of the name is agreed upon by most, but it's far more likely the stew was created much earlier. With the original ingredients of game (usually squirrel) and corn, and long simmering over an open fire, it's typical of early native dishes.

- In Dutch oven, combine chicken, beef and pork; add water to cover. Bring to a boil; cover, reduce heat and simmer 2 hours or until chicken and meats are tender.

- Strain stock, reserving chicken and meats. Let chicken and meats cool.

- Skin, bone and coarsely chop chicken. Coarsely chop beef and pork.

- Skim fat from stock, reserving 7 cups stock. Reserve any remaining stock for another use, if desired.

- Combine stock, chicken, meats, tomatoes, tomato paste, corn, potatoes, peppers, lima beans, onion, carrots, okra, green peas and cabbage; bring to a boil. Cover and reduce heat; simmer 2 hours.

- Stir in sugar, Worcestershire sauce, lemon juice, salt and pepper just before serving.

2 gallons

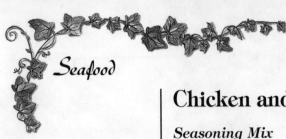

Jambalaya, a Cajun/
Creole dish, is perhaps
the most versatile main
dish the South has to
offer. There's something
about serving jambalaya
at a party that almost
guarantees the good
times will roll. As it's
difficult to decide just
what kind of jambalaya
to make (meat, shellfish,
or poultry), we normally
put a little bit of
everything into the pot.
(Not one to complicate
matters, but you can use
1 cup chopped smoked
ham instead of the
sausage. Or you could
stir in ½ pound cooked
crabmeat at the end to
replace the shrimp.)

Chicken and Seafood Jambalaya

Seasoning Mix
2   bay leaves
1½ teaspoons each: salt, cayenne pepper, dried oregano
1¼ teaspoons each: black pepper, white pepper
¾   teaspoon dried thyme

- Blend spices for seasoning mix and set aside.

Jambalaya
2½ tablespoons bacon fat or lard
⅔   cup chopped tasso
⅔   cup chopped andouille sausage
1½ cups chopped onion
1   cup chopped celery
¾   cup chopped green bell pepper
1   chopped jalapeño pepper
1   cup raw chicken, diced
    Seasoning mix
1½ teaspoons minced garlic
4   tomatoes, peeled and chopped
¾   cup tomato sauce
2   cups chicken stock
½   cup chopped green onions
1   cup rice, uncooked
½   pound peeled shrimp
½   pound shucked oysters (or equal amount of crab)

- Preheat oven to 350°.
- Melt bacon fat over medium heat in large sauté pan and add tasso or ham and sausage.
- Sauté 5 to 8 minutes, stirring frequently.
- Add chopped onions, celery, bell peppers and jalapeño. Sauté until tender but firm.
- Add chicken; increase heat and cook 1 minute, stirring.
- Reduce heat to medium, add seasoning mix and garlic. Simmer 5 minutes; add tomatoes.

Chicken and Seafood Jambalaya *continued*

- Cook until chicken is tender, about 8 to 10 minutes, stirring frequently.
- Add tomato sauce and stir 5 minutes. Add chicken stock; bring to a boil; add chopped green onions.
- Simmer an additional 2 minutes.
- Add uncooked rice, shrimp and oysters; stir and remove from heat.
- Pour jambalaya into 9 x 13 inch, ungreased baking pan and bake 30 minutes, until rice is tender.
- Remove bay leaves and serve.

Serves 8

Seafood Fantasy

1   **(10 ounce) package frozen spinach**
1   **(10¾ ounce) can cream of mushroom soup**
¼   **cup all-purpose flour**
½   **cup milk**
1   **(4 ounce) can mushrooms, drained**
1   **cup shredded Swiss cheese**
2   **(7 ounce) cans crabmeat, drained and flaked**
¼   **cup roasted almonds, chopped**
¼   **cup white wine**
2   **tablespoons butter**
1   **cup bread crumbs**

- Preheat oven to 400°.
- Cook and drain spinach. Spread over bottom of greased 2 quart casserole.
- Combine soup, flour, milk and mushrooms in saucepan; cook until thickened.
- Add cheese and stir until melted.
- Stir in crabmeat, almonds and wine; pour over spinach.
- Melt butter in small skillet; add bread crumbs. Sprinkle over mixture.

Serves 6

Shrimp is also delicious.

Crabmeat Au Gratin

½   pound onions (1 large white, some green)
3   ribs celery, diced
½   pound butter
4   tablespoons all-purpose flour
1   (10 ounce) can milk
1   (5 ounce) can milk
2   egg yolks, beaten
2   pounds fresh white crabmeat
     Salt and pepper to taste
10 ounces mild grated Cheddar cheese, divided

- Preheat oven to 350°.
- Sauté onions and celery in butter until soft.
- Add flour and blend.
- Add milk and blend, stirring constantly.
- Remove from heat; add egg yolks, crabmeat, salt, pepper and half of the cheese; mix well.
- Put in greased 11 x 7 casserole dish and top with remaining cheese.
- Bake uncovered for 20 minutes.

Serves 6 to 8

Blackened Salmon with Mango Salsa

Try this dish for an intense, flavor-packed dish that's easy to make.

2	**(6 ounce) salmon fillets**
	Cooking spray
¼	**teaspoon salt**
1	**tablespoon blackened seasoning**
	Oil for frying

- Spray salmon evenly with spray.
- Sprinkle evenly with salt and seasoning.
- Heat oil in large skillet over medium-high heat. Place salmon in skillet; cook 4 to 6 minutes on each side or to desired degree of doneness.
- Serve fillets with Mango Salsa (recipe to right).

Mango Salsa

1	large, ripe mango, peeled and coarsely chopped
¼	cup finely chopped purple onion
2	tablespoons chopped fresh cilantro
3	tablespoons orange juice
1	jalapeño pepper, seeded and minced
¼	teaspoon ground cumin
¼	teaspoon salt

- Stir together mango, onion, cilantro, orange juice, jalapeño pepper, cumin and salt.
- Chill if desired.
- Serve salmon immediately with salsa.

Serves 2

Salmon Fillets in Lemon Sauce

¾	**cup lemon juice**
3	**tablespoons finely chopped onion**
	Salt and pepper to taste
1½	**tablespoons light brown sugar**
1	**teaspoon dry mustard**
1	**pound salmon fillets (skinned and cut in 4-inch pieces)**
2	**tablespoons parsley, chopped**

- In small saucepan, combine lemon juice, onion, salt, pepper, brown sugar and mustard; bring to a boil.
- Place salmon on foil lined pan; pour sauce over fillets.
- Broil about 15 minutes basting frequently with sauce.
- When done, serve with parsley sprinkled over top.

Serves 4

This may be served with pasta tossed with remaining lemon sauce.

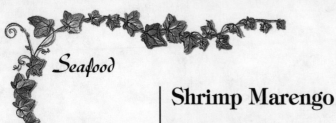

Shrimp Marengo

8 slices bacon, diced
1 cup diced onion
1 clove garlic, minced
3 pounds shrimp, cooked, peeled and deveined
2 (8 ounce) cans mushroom stems and pieces, undrained
4 cups canned tomatoes
1 (6 ounce) can tomato paste
1 (15½ ounce) can beef consommé
1 teaspoon dried basil
1¼ teaspoons dried oregano
1 teaspoon salt
1 teaspoon Accent
1 tablespoon sugar
3 tablespoons prepared mustard
3 drops Tabasco sauce
½ cup all-purpose flour
½ cup water
Cooked rice

- In a very large skillet, fry bacon until crisp. Set aside.
- To bacon drippings, add onion and cook lightly.
- Add garlic, shrimp, mushrooms, tomatoes, tomato paste, consommé, basil, oregano, salt, Accent, sugar, mustard and Tabasco.
- Simmer for about 10 minutes.
- Combine flour and water to make smooth paste. Stir into mixture and cook 1 minute, stirring constantly.
- Serve over cooked rice.

Serves 16

Shrimp Creole

⅓ **cup shortening**
¼ **cup flour**
1 **pound peeled, deveined raw shrimp**
1 **garlic clove, minced**
½ **cup minced onion**
2 **tablespoons minced parsley**
½ **cup chopped green pepper**
1 **cup water**
2 **teaspoons salt**
2 **bay leaves**
¼ **teaspoon cayenne pepper**
1 **(8 ounce) can tomato sauce**
   Cooked rice

"Every one was just great. I don't know how we could have coped without such a wonderful group. Thanks to all of you."

- Melt shortening in heavy skillet over high heat.
- Add flour and stir until it is light brown.
- Lower heat; add shrimp; cook 3 minutes or until pink.
- Add garlic, onion, parsley and green pepper; cook 2 minutes longer.
- Raise heat; gradually add water, then salt, bay leaves, pepper and tomato sauce.
- Bring to a boil; simmer for 20 to 30 minutes covered.
- Serve very hot over fluffy, cooked rice.

Serves 4

To reduce fat, omit shortening and brown flour on flat cookie sheet for 20 minutes in 400° oven stirring flour every few minutes.

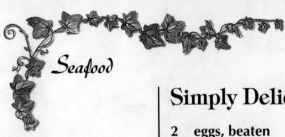

Simply Delicious Crab Cakes

To get to the crabmeat, first pry off the apron or tail flap. Lift off the top shell, holding the crab in the space left by removing the apron. Pull and discard the feathery gills beneath the top shell. Twist off claws where attached to body. Discard stomach mass. Twist off legs. Crack claws and legs with seafood or nut crackers. Remove meat with a cocktail fork.

2 **eggs, beaten**
1/3 **cup bread crumbs**
2 **tablespoons mayonnaise**
Juice of 1/2 lemon
1 **teaspoon Worcestershire sauce**
1 **teaspoon dry mustard**
1/2 **teaspoon salt**
1/4 **teaspoon pepper**
Hot sauce (optional)
1 **pound crabmeat, cooked**
1/3 **cup bread crumbs**
1 **stick butter**

- In large bowl, blend eggs, bread crumbs, mayonnaise, lemon juice, Worcestershire sauce, dry mustard, salt and pepper. Stir in crabmeat and mix well.
- Shape into patties and roll in bread crumbs.
- In large skillet, melt butter and brown crab cakes about 4 minutes on both sides.
- Drain on paper towel before serving.

Serves 4

Frogmore Stew

3 tablespoons prepared shrimp boil
3 tablespoons salt
1½ gallons water
2 pounds hot smoked link sausage or kielbasa, cut into 2 inch pieces
12 ears freshly shucked corn, broken into 3 to 4 inch pieces
4 pounds shrimp, unpeeled

- In a very large stockpot, add the shrimp boil and salt to the water and bring to a boil.
- Add the sausage and boil, uncovered, for 5 minutes.
- Add the corn and cook 5 minutes.
- Add the shrimp and cook for 3 minutes (don't wait for the liquid to return to a boil before timing the corn and shrimp.)
- Drain immediately and serve.

Serves 8

Leftover Frogmore Stew helps make delicious soup. Peel the shrimp, cut the corn from the cob, slice the sausage thinly, then add to simmering tomato juice to warm through. Season with fresh hot peppers.

St. Helena Island, near Hilton Head, used to have a town center called Frogmore, named after an ancestral English country estate. It consisted of four buildings, including the post office; new residents have changed the official name to St. Helena. In the early twentieth century, Frogmore was the site of booming caviar and diamondback terrapin businesses. The "stew" is named after the old Sea Island settlement.

This Lowcountry seafood boil is usually served on paper plates around newspaper-covered picnic tables outdoors, with plenty of cold beer. When finished eating, just discard the newspapers with the shells and corn cobs wrapped inside. The recipe may be adjusted for more or fewer people by allowing ½ pound of shrimp per person, ¼ pound of sausage per person, 1 ½ ears of corn per person, and 2 tablespoons of shrimp seasoning per gallon of water.

Steak Marinade

1	cup bourbon
1	pound brown sugar
½	cup lemon juice
1	onion, chopped
1	tablespoon minced garlic
1	cup soy sauce

- Combine bourbon, sugar, lemon juice, onion, garlic and soy sauce; stir until completely mixed.

1 quart

Marinate no longer than 6 to 8 hours before cooking.

Sonny Tuck's Barbeque Sauce

1	quart white vinegar
1	pint corn oil (must use corn)
4½	ounces mustard
1	tablespoon onion salt
2½	ounces Worcestershire sauce
6-7	ounces sugar
½	cup salt
7	ounces ketchup
2	teaspoons black pepper
	Dash garlic powder
	Dash Tabasco sauce

- Thoroughly blend all ingredients.

2 quarts

This is a great sauce to use when roasting a whole pig. You may use a ladle or a cotton mop.

Chicken Marinade

1½ cups vegetable oil
¾   cup soy sauce
¼   cup Worcestershire sauce
2   tablespoons dry mustard
2¼ teaspoons salt
1   teaspoon black pepper
½   cup white wine vinegar
1½ tablespoons parsley flakes
2   garlic cloves, minced
⅓   cup lemon juice

- Combine oil, soy sauce, Worcestershire sauce, mustard, salt, pepper, vinegar, parsley flakes, garlic and lemon juice in a 1 quart jar. Keep refrigerated.
- Marinate meat at least 8 hours; better if overnight.
- Marinade is good for any type meat.

1 quart

"We appreciate your help and hope you continue for a long time. God Bless You."

Raisin Sauce

½ cup seedless raisins
½ cup water
⅓ cup port wine
½ teaspoon grated orange zest
⅓ cup orange juice
¼ cup brown sugar, packed firm
1 tablespoon cornstarch
   Salt to taste
   Dash allspice

- Rinse raisins; place in medium saucepan.
- Add water, wine, zest and orange juice. Heat to boiling.
- Blend sugar with cornstarch, salt and allspice; stir into orange mixture.
- Cook, stirring constantly until clear.

1⅓ cups

Serve hot over ham or pork chops.

Side Dishes

Side Dishes

Linguine Carbonara

Strips of prosciutto ham and crisp bacon toss meaty flavor into this creamy, rich pasta dish.

½	**pound bacon, cut into 1 inch pieces**
¼	**cup olive oil**
1	**medium onion, chopped**
1	**cup chopped fresh parsley (about 1 bunch)**
4	**ounces fontina cheese, cubed**
3	**ounces prosciutto, cut into thin strips**
1	**(1 pound) package dried linguine or spaghetti**
4	**egg yolks, lightly beaten**
¾	**cup half-and-half, heated**
1	**teaspoon salt**
	Freshly ground pepper to taste
1	**cup freshly grated Parmesan cheese, divided**
	Fresh parsley sprigs for garnish

- Fry bacon in a large skillet over medium heat until crisp. Drain on paper towels. Pour off drippings.

- Add oil and onion to skillet; sauté until onion is tender. Set aside.

- In a small bowl, combine parsley, fontina cheese and prosciutto. Set aside.

- In a Dutch oven, cook linguine according to package directions; drain.

- Return to Dutch oven; immediately stir in egg yolks. Add bacon, onion, parsley mixture, heated half-and-half, salt, pepper and ½ cup Parmesan cheese. Cook over low heat until thoroughly heated, stirring constantly; transfer to serving dish.

- Sprinkle with remaining ½ cup Parmesan cheese. Garnish, if desired. Serve immediately.

Serves 8

Pasta may have originated in Italy, but surely a Southerner would have invented it soon if an Italian hadn't. Pasta comes in many shapes and sizes; the size determines the cooking time. The test for doneness is the same - *"al dente"* - as they say in Italy. This simply means "to the tooth." When cooked properly, pasta should be pliable but firm and no longer starchy.

Cooking With Care 139

Macaroni and Cheese

1   (8 ounce) box macaroni
1   egg
1   (8 ounce) carton sour cream
1   (12 ounce) carton cottage cheese
3   cups shredded sharp Cheddar cheese, divided
Salt and pepper
Paprika
Melted butter, as desired

Macaroni and cheese: Food for the soul. It probably wouldn't be on the menu for your mother-in-law's first visit, and it isn't exactly gourmet fare, but it is one of the most popular-if not the most popular-American comfort foods. Nearly every soul food cookbook and many Southern cookbooks have recipes for this favorite; with few differences from one to the next.

- Preheat oven to 350°.
- In medium saucepan, cook macaroni according to package directions. Place in a greased 11 x 7 inch baking dish.
- In large mixing bowl, whisk egg. Add sour cream, cottage cheese, 2 cups Cheddar cheese, salt and pepper. Pour over macaroni.
- Sprinkle remaining Cheddar cheese over macaroni mixture.
- Pour butter over cheese. Sprinkle generous amount of paprika all over top.
- Bake for 35 minutes.

Serves 6 to 8

Creamy Chicken Manicotti

8	manicotti shells
1	(10¾ ounce) can creamy chicken mushroom soup, undiluted
½	cup sour cream
2	cups chopped cooked chicken
¼	cup minced onion
2	tablespoons butter or margarine
1	(4 ounce) can sliced mushrooms, undrained
1	cup shredded Monterey Jack cheese

- Preheat oven to 350°.
- Cook manicotti shells according to package directions; drain and set aside.
- Combine soup and sour cream; stir well.
- Combine half of soup mixture and chicken; stir well.
- Stuff manicotti shells with chicken mixture; place in a greased 12 x 8 inch baking dish.
- Sauté onion in butter in a large skillet until tender; add mushrooms.
- Stir reserved soup mixture into mushroom mixture.
- Spoon over manicotti; bake uncovered for 15 minutes. Sprinkle with cheese and bake an additional 5 minutes.

Serves 4

Layered Shells Florentine

1   (7 ounce) package small shells
1   (10 ounce) package frozen chopped spinach, thawed and squeezed dry
1¾ cups cottage cheese or ricotta cheese
1   egg, slightly beaten
¼   cup grated Parmesan cheese
1   cup shredded mozzarella cheese, divided
⅓   cup chopped fresh parsley
    Salt and pepper to taste
1   (28 ounce) jar spaghetti sauce, divided

- Preheat oven to 350°.
- In medium saucepan, cook pasta according to package directions. Set aside.
- In large bowl, stir together spinach, cottage or ricotta cheese, egg, Parmesan cheese, ⅔ cup mozzarella, parsley, salt and pepper.
- Toss hot pasta with 2½ cups sauce. Arrange half in bottom of 13 x 9 inch greased baking dish.
- Layer spinach mixture over pasta.
- Cover with remaining pasta.
- Spread remaining sauce over top. Sprinkle with remaining mozzarella cheese and additional Parmesan cheese.
- Bake 35 to 40 minutes until bubbly.

Serves 6 to 8

Three-Cheese Chicken Pasta Bake

Layers of pasta, cheeses and chicken make this dish similar to a traditional baked lasagne. A real treat for calorie watchers at only 318 calories/serving.

vases (ollas), squash pots and melon vessels. The colection contains several important examples of Navaho woolen textile art. Navajo Indian weavings have aways been treasured for thier excellence of craftsmanship.

8	ounces lasagne noodles
½	cup chopped onion
½	cup chopped green bell pepper
3	tablespoons butter or margarine
1	(10¾ ounce) can cream of chicken soup
1	(4 ounce) can sliced mushrooms, drained
½	cup diced pimiento, drained
⅓	cup skim milk
½	teaspoon dried basil, crushed
1½	cups low-fat cottage cheese, divided
2	cups chopped turkey or chicken
1½	cups shredded American cheese, divided
½	cup grated Parmesan cheese, divided

- Preheat oven to 350°.
- In large pan, cook lasagne noodles according to package directions. Drain well.
- In small skillet, sauté onion and green pepper in butter or margarine until tender.
- Stir in mushrooms, soup, pimiento, milk and basil. Mix well.
- Layer half of the noodles in a greased 13 x 9 inch baking dish; top with half each of the soup mixture, cottage cheese, chicken, ¾ cup American cheese and ¼ cup Parmesan cheese.
- Repeat second layer with noodles, soup mixture, cottage cheese and chicken.
- Bake for 45 minutes covered. Remove cover; top with ¾ cup American cheese and ¼ cup Parmesan cheese.
- Bake an additional 2 minutes or until cheeses are melted.

Serves 10

Chicken Tetrazzini

3   slices bacon
1   small onion, chopped
½   green bell pepper, chopped
¼   cup milk
1   (10¾ ounce) can cream of mushroom soup, undiluted
1   (8 ounce) loaf pasteurized prepared cheese product, cubed
2   cups chopped, cooked turkey or chicken
8   ounces spaghetti, cooked
1   (2 ounce) jar diced pimiento, drained

- Preheat oven to 375°.
- In a skillet, fry bacon until crisp; drain, reserving 2 tablespoons drippings in pan. Crumble bacon; set aside.
- Add onion and bell pepper to drippings; sauté 2 minutes or until tender.
- Stir in milk, soup and cheese; stirring constantly until blended.
- Stir in chicken, spaghetti and pimiento. Spoon into a lightly greased 2 quart baking dish.
- Bake for 30 minutes or until thoroughly heated. Sprinkle with reserved bacon.

Serves 4

Wild Rice Casserole

¾   **cup wild rice**
½   **pound bacon, fried and crumbled (save drippings)**
1   **cup celery, sliced thin**
1   **cup onion, diced**
½   **cup green pepper, diced**
1   **(4 ounce) can sliced mushrooms, drained**
½   **pound pork sausage, browned and drained**
1   **(10¾ ounce) can cream of mushroom soup**
5   **ounces water**
1   **teaspoon salt**
2   **teaspoons soy sauce**
3   **tablespoons butter**

- Preheat oven to 325°.
- Wash rice thoroughly; bring to a boil; drain.
- Add water and bring to a boil again; drain.
- Place rice in greased 3 quart casserole dish.
- Fry bacon in large skillet; remove bacon and set aside.
- Sauté celery, onions, green peppers and mushrooms in bacon drippings; drain remaining drippings. Drain and add to the rice.
- Brown sausage and drain on paper towels.
- In small bowl, mix soup, water, salt and soy sauce together.
- Combine bacon, sausage and soup mixture together; add to rice and mix well.
- Pat butter on top; cover and bake 1½ hours.

Serves 4 to 6

From a parsimonious platter of hoppin' John to a sophisticated seafood pilau, rice has been an inspiration to Southern cooks of every social strata. In the deep South, rice served the same purpose as did the potato in the upper South. It is a perfect accompaniment to seafood, meats, soups and stews. Barbequed hash, another Southern favorite, is served over white rice. In addition to white rice, there are other types of rice: parboiled, precooked; brown and wild rice.

Traditional Hoppin' John

4 slices bacon, diced
⅓ cup diced carrots
½ cup finely chopped celery
¼ cup finely diced onion
10 ounces fresh or frozen black-eyed peas
1 whole garlic clove
2¾ cups water, approximately, divided
1 bay leaf
Salt to taste
¼ teaspoon dried hot red pepper flakes
2 cups cooked rice
Cheddar cheese as desired
1 cup finely chopped scallions

- In small saucepan, fry bacon until crisp. Add the carrots, celery and onion and cook about 1 minute.
- Add the peas, garlic, about 1¼ cups of the water, or to barely cover, bay leaf, salt and red pepper flakes. Bring to a boil and let simmer, uncovered 30 to 40 minutes, until tender but not mushy. Remove from heat.
- Arrange hot rice in the center of a platter. Spoon the hot pea mixture, including liquid, over the rice. You may garnish with cheese and chopped scallions.

Serves 4 to 6

Hoppin' John is one of the most traditional Southern dishes. It is served in many Southern homes on New Year's Day; eating it on this holiday is said to bring those that partake good luck for the entire year.

Veggie Wild Rice

1   **(14 ounce) can vegetable broth**
¾   **cup water**
1   **(6 ounce) package long-grain and wild rice mix**
1   **tablespoon olive oil**
3   **tablespoons chopped walnuts**
½   **medium red pepper, chopped**
1   **cup fresh mushrooms, sliced**
1   **clove garlic, minced**
3   **green onions, sliced**
¼   **teaspoon salt**
    Fresh ground pepper to taste

- Bring broth and water to a full boil in medium saucepan.
- Add rice mix (discard seasoning packet). Cover and reduce heat; simmer 30 minutes.
- Heat olive oil in large skillet; sauté walnuts for 5 minutes.
- Remove from pan; set aside.
- Add red pepper, mushrooms and garlic to skillet; sauté 5 minutes or until tender.
- Stir in cooked rice, green onions, salt and pepper.
- Sprinkle with walnuts.

Serves 6

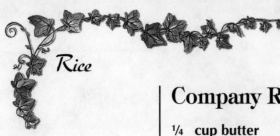

"…how fortunate we were to see how caring and devoted everyone at hospice is, toward not only to the patient, but to the family as well. May God richly bless you."

Company Rice

¼   **cup butter**
⅓   **cup wild rice**
⅔   **cup brown rice**
8   **ounces fresh mushrooms, cleaned and sliced**
3   **green onions, sliced**
½   **teaspoon salt**
1   **(14½ ounce) can chicken broth**
2   **tablespoons cooking sherry**
½   **cup sliced almonds, toasted**

- In large skillet, melt butter over medium heat. Add wild and brown rice, stirring occasionally for 5 minutes.
- Add mushrooms, green onions, salt, chicken broth and sherry.
- Bring to a boil, cover and reduce heat; simmer 1 hour and 5 minutes or until rice is done.
- Drain excess liquid and fluff with fork.
- Sprinkle with almonds.

Serves 6 to 8

Crockpot Broccoli and Rice Casserole

1   small onion, diced
¼   cup margarine, melted
2   cups quick-cooking rice
2   cups water
1   (10 ounce) can cream of mushroom soup
½   teaspoon salt
1   (5 ounce jar) sharp cheese spread
1   (10 ounce) package frozen chopped broccoli, partially thawed
    Cornflake crumbs for topping
    Butter to brown crumbs

- Combine onion, margarine, rice, water, soup, salt, cheese spread and broccoli; mix thoroughly.
- Put in greased 4-quart crockpot.
- Cook covered on low for 7 to 10 hours (high for 2 to 3 hours)
- Brown cornflake crumbs in butter; just before serving, sprinkle with buttered crumbs.

Serves 4 to 6

Butter Beans, Bacon and Tomatoes

3	slices bacon, chopped
1	medium onion, finely chopped
1	medium green bell pepper, chopped
3	garlic cloves, minced
2	bay leaves
4	tomatoes, skinned and diced
4	cups chicken broth
4	cups fresh or frozen butter beans, thawed
2	tablespoons parsley
	Salt and pepper to taste
1	teaspoon Worcestershire sauce
½-1	teaspoon hot sauce

- Fry bacon in a Dutch oven until crisp.
- Add onion, pepper and garlic; sauté until vegetables are tender.
- Stir in bay leaves and tomato and cook 3 minutes.
- Stir in broth and butter beans; bring to a boil.
- Cover, reduce heat and simmer, stirring occasionally for 30 minutes.
- Simmer uncovered 20 minutes, stirring often.
- Stir in parsley, salt, pepper, Worcestershire sauce and hot sauce.
- Simmer 5 minutes, stirring often. Discard bay leaves.

Serves 6 to 8

Southern Collard Greens

Mustard and turnip greens can be substituted for the collards.

1 **pound salt pork or smoked pork shoulder**
3 **quarts water**
   Pepper to taste
4 **pounds greens of your choice**

- Slice salt pork at ½ inch intervals, don't cut completely through.
- Add meat and pepper to water and bring to a boil in large Dutch oven.
- Cover, reduce heat and simmer 1 hour.
- While meat is cooking, remove stems and discolored spots from greens. Wash thoroughly; drain and slice into strips.
- Add greens to meat and cook 20 to 30 minutes.
- Serve using slotted spoon.

Serves 4 to 5

There is no vegetable more Southern than greens, no food dearer to the soul of the Lowcountry. Collards, spinach, mustard and turnip greens are some of the commonly used greens to grace the tables of Southerners, rich and poor alike. Greens usually release most of their bitterness after 10 minutes of cooking in boiling water. Longer cooking creates a richer tasting "pot likker." Collards have strong personalities; put together with ham, candied sweet potatoes, black-eyed peas, fried chicken and plenty of cornbread to sponge up the "pot likker," you have a traditional Southern meal.

Buttermilk Fried Corn

3 **cups fresh corn**
2¼ **cups buttermilk**
1 **cup all-purpose flour**
1 **cup cornmeal**
   Salt and pepper to taste
   Corn oil

- Stir together corn and buttermilk; let sit 30 minutes. Drain corn.
- Combine flour, cornmeal, salt and pepper in large zip top bag.
- Add corn to flour mixture, a little at a time, and shake to coat.
- Pour 1 inch oil in Dutch oven; heat to 375°.
- Fry corn in small batches 2 minutes or until golden brown.
- Drain on paper towels.

Serves 6 to 8

Fried Okra

1	pound fresh okra, washed
2	cups buttermilk
1	cup white cornmeal
1	cup self-rising flour
	Salt to taste
¼	teaspoon cayenne pepper
	Oil for frying
	Bacon drippings

- Cut off stem and tips from okra; cut okra into ½-inch pieces.
- Add okra to buttermilk, cover and chill 30 minutes.
- Combine cornmeal, flour, salt and cayenne pepper in a bowl or bag.
- Remove okra from buttermilk with slotted spoon. Dredge or shake okra in flour mixture.
- Pour oil and bacon drippings to equal 2 inches in heavy skillet or Dutch oven; heat to 375°.
- Fry okra (in batches) about 4 minutes or until golden brown.

Serves 4 to 6

Vegetables

Fried Okra Patties

1½ cups okra, thinly sliced
2 tablespoons buttermilk
3 tablespoons all-purpose flour
2 tablespoons cornmeal
1 teaspoon salt
⅛ teaspoon pepper
1 egg, beaten
Cooking oil

- Mix okra, buttermilk, flour, cornmeal, salt, pepper and egg together.
- Heat oil to 375° in heavy skillet.
- Drop okra into oil by tablespoonful and fry until golden brown (about 4 minutes).

Serves 2 to 3

Although there are many ideas on where okra originates, many say it is from India or Africa. Because of its somewhat slimy quality, okra is really a love-it or loathe-it vegetable. However, when whole okra is fried, pickled or sautéed this characteristic is virtually nonexistent. Okra and tomatoes over rice, gumbo and fried are some of the ways Southerners enjoy them. Buy okra no longer than your finger-bright green, unblemished, and all uniform in size. Trim the caps from the pods as closely as possible without cutting into the pod itself so that the pod remains whole in cooking.

Parmesan Onion Bake

6   medium onions, sliced fairly thin
1   cup diced celery
8   tablespoons butter, divided
¼   cup all-purpose flour
1   teaspoon salt
     Pepper to taste
1½ cups milk
⅓   cup grated Parmesan cheese
½   cup chopped pecans

- Preheat oven to 350°.
- In large skillet, sauté onions and celery in 3 tablespoons butter until tender; drain and set aside.
- In saucepan, melt remaining butter; stir in all-purpose flour, salt and pepper until smooth.
- Gradually stir in milk. Bring to a boil; cook and stir for about 2 minutes until thickened.
- Pour over vegetables; toss to coat.
- Pour into an ungreased 2 quart baking dish.
- Sprinkle with cheese and pecans.
- Bake for 20 to 25 minutes or until heated through.

Serves 6 to 8

Vidalia Onion Pie

1   (9-inch) pie shell
2   pounds Vidalia onions or other sweet onion
1   stick butter or margarine, melted
3   eggs, beaten
1   cup sour cream
¼   teaspoon salt
¼   teaspoon white pepper
     Dash Tabasco sauce
     Parmesan cheese

- Preheat oven to 450°.
- Bake pie shell until light brown.
- Combine onions, butter, eggs, sour cream, salt, pepper and Tabasco sauce.
- Pour into pie shell and top with Parmesan cheese.
- Bake 15 minutes then reduce heat to 325°; bake for another 15 to 20 minutes.

Serves 6

New Potato Casserole

10   medium new red potatoes
½   cup grated Cheddar cheese
1   cup mayonnaise
½   cup chopped onion
1   pound bacon, cooked and crumbled

- Preheat oven to 350°.
- Boil unpeeled potatoes; slice.
- Combine cheese, mayonnaise and onion; gently stir into potatoes.
- Place in a greased 2 quart casserole and top with bacon.
- Bake for 20 to 30 minutes or until bubbly.

Serves 6 to 8

The Sweet Vidalia Onion

Georgians take great pride in the onion from Vidalia. This sweet onion can be eaten like fruit. The sugar content is comparable to that of an apple, or a bottle of cola. This onion can be eaten with a variety of foods or just raw. The soil and climate of Vidalia, Georgia contribute to the sweet taste.

The Vidalia onion story started in 1931 when a farmer discovered the onions he had planted weren't hot, but sweet, and he sold them for $3.50 per 50 pound bag. This was during the Great Depression days, so the price was high. Other farmers followed suit. Eventually, the Vidalia onion was named the official vegetable of Georgia. Today, 70 million pounds of these onions can be stored in a controlled atmosphere for up to 6 months, extending onion sales into the fall holiday season. Vidalia's delicate nature requires that they be harvested by hand, thoroughly dried and treated gently during grading and packaging.

Party Potatoes

¼ cup margarine
1 medium onion, chopped
3 tablespoons chopped green pepper
1 tablespoon chopped pimento
2½ tablespoons all-purpose flour
2 cups milk
5 cups cubed, cooked potatoes
   Salt and pepper to taste
2 cups shredded Cheddar cheese

- Preheat oven to 350°.
- Sauté onion and green pepper in margarine for 5 minutes.
- Add pimento and flour. Toss gently.
- Slowly stir in milk and cook until thickened.
- Add potatoes, salt and pepper.
- Pour into a greased 9 x 13 inch casserole dish.
- Top with cheese.
- Bake for 30 minutes.

Serves 8 to 12

This dish can be combined the day before, refrigerated and baked when ready to serve.

Foiled Potatoes to Go

10 Small white or red potatoes (more if needed), scrubbed
Aluminum foil
Salt and pepper to taste
Butter as desired

- Boil potatoes wrapped in foil in salted water.
- Drain water; carefully unwrap potatoes.
- Rub with butter; salt and pepper. Rewrap potatoes.
- Place in dish with lid to keep warm and off you go.

Serves 6 to 8

Spinach with Mushrooms Caps

1   pound fresh mushrooms
½   cup butter, divided
¼   cup diced onion
1   clove garlic, minced
2   (10½ ounce) packages frozen spinach, cooked and drained well
1   cup shredded Cheddar cheese, divided

- Preheat oven to 350°.
- Wash mushrooms and snap off stems from caps. Save stems.
- Sauté caps in ¼ cup butter until brown; remove and pour off liquid.
- Sauté diced mushroom stems, onion and garlic in other ¼ cup of butter.
- Combine spinach, onion mixture, salt and pepper.
- Put in shallow, greased 10-inch casserole dish.
- Sprinkle with ½ cup cheese.
- Arrange mushroom caps over spinach. Cover with remaining cheese.
- Bake 20 to 30 minutes until bubbly.

Serves 4 to 6

Corn Pudding

3   eggs
1   cup whipping cream
1   (15¼ ounce) can creamed corn
2   (15¼ ounce) cans whole kernel corn, drained
½   cup butter, melted
4½ teaspoons all-purpose flour
2   tablespoons sugar
1   teaspoon baking powder
     Salt and pepper to taste

- Preheat oven to 350°.
- In large bowl, beat eggs and cream.
- Add corn and butter.
- Combine all-purpose flour, sugar, baking powder, salt and pepper; stir into corn mixture.
- Pour into greased 1½ quart baking dish.
- Bake uncovered for 45 to 55 minutes until set and golden brown.

Serves 4 to 6

Creamy Squash Casserole

1½ **pounds yellow squash, peeled, seeded and cubed**
1   **medium onion, chopped**
1   **(10¾ ounce) can cream of chicken soup**
1   **(8 ounce) carton sour cream**
1   **(4 ounce) jar pimento, chopped**
1   **(8½ ounce) can water chestnuts, chopped**
1   **(8 ounce) package herb stuffing mix**
1   **stick margarine, melted**

- Preheat oven to 350°.
- Cook squash and onions in salted water until tender. Drain well.
- Add soup, sour cream, pimento and water chestnuts.
- Butter 2 quart casserole dish and put some of the stuffing mix in bottom.
- Spread squash mixture on top.
- Add margarine to the remainder of stuffing mix; mix well.
- Place stuffing on top of casserole.
- Bake for 35 to 40 minutes.

Serves 4 to 6

May use crushed Ritz crackers in place of stuffing mix.

"Every day in the world around us, real-life angels are doing the things they do…and bringing more smiles to the world around them…"

Tomato Pie

1	**(9 inch) pie shell, baked and cooled**
4-6	**medium tomatoes, blanched, peeled and thickly sliced**
1	**small onion, diced**
1	**tablespoon margarine**
2	**tablespoons mayonnaise**
1	**teaspoon oregano**
2	**cups grated mozzarella cheese, divided**

- Preheat oven to 350°.
- Drain tomatoes. Put half of the tomatoes in pie shell. Set aside.
- Sauté onion in margarine.
- Combine onion with mayonnaise and oregano; mix well.
- Spread onion mixture on top of tomatoes.
- Sprinkle with 1 cup cheese.
- Place remaining tomatoes on top of cheese.
- Sprinkle with remaining cheese.
- Cover loosely with foil and bake for 20 minutes.
- Remove foil and bake an additional 10 minutes.

Serves 6

Park Seed Company

George W. Park was born on a farm near Fannettburg, PA. When he was a child, his mother noticed his interest in horticulture and encouraged him to raise flowers in a corner of her garden. From that beginning grew Park Seed Co., Inc., of Greenwood which today offers the broadest range of horticultural products in America. Park's first catalog, published in 1868, was just 8 pages and used 2 illustrations, wood engravings of an aster and a pansy. In 1871, he started a monthly magazine offering advice on gardening and creating a forum where people could share gardening experiences. In 1984, millions of Park's tomato seeds were a part of NASA's first commercial payload aboard a space shuttle. The cargo remained in orbit for 5 years, and in 1989, the seeds were

Garlic Mashed Potatoes

*Don't let the amount of garlic fool you. These potatoes are
fantastic!*

10-12	**medium red potatoes, cubed**
8-10	**garlic cloves, peeled (don't mince)**
1	**stick butter**
	Heavy cream to get consistency desired

- Boil potatoes and garlic cloves together about 20 to 30 minutes or until tender.
- Drain and return potatoes and garlic to pan; add butter and cream.
- Mix by hand or with potato masher (not electric mixer); mixture will be lumpy. Add salt and pepper to taste.

Serves 4 to 6

Asparagus Casserole

24	**round buttery crackers, crushed, divided**
2	**(15½ ounce) cans asparagus spears, drained (save juice)**
4	**hard-boiled eggs, sliced**
¾	**pound sharp Cheddar cheese, grated**
2	**(10¾ ounce) cans cream of mushroom soup**
¾	**cup milk**

- Preheat oven to 375°.
- Spread ⅓ cracker crumbs on bottom of greased 3-quart baking dish.
- Place layer of asparagus spears, eggs and cheese over crumbs.
- Sprinkle ⅓ cracker crumbs over first layer.
- Repeat first layer until asparagus, eggs and cheese are used.
- Mix soup and milk.
- Pour this mixture over vegetable mixture.
- Top with remaining cracker crumbs.
- Bake 1 hour uncovered.

Serves 8 to 10

distributed to more than
3,000,000 students for
use in science
experiments.

Two-Tone Twice Baked Potatoes

6   medium russet potatoes, scrubbed
6   medium sweet potatoes, scrubbed
⅔   cup sour cream, divided
⅓   cup milk
1   cup shredded Cheddar cheese
2   tablespoons minced chives
**   Salt and pepper to taste, divided**

- Pierce all potatoes with fork.
- Bake at 400° for 60 to 70 minutes or until tender.
- Set sweet potatoes aside.
- Slice a third off the top of each russet potato; scoop out pulp, leaving skins intact.
- Place pulp in bowl; mash with ⅓ cup sour cream, milk, cheese, chives, salt and pepper. Set aside.
- Cut off top of each sweet potato; scoop out pulp, leaving skins intact. Mash pulp with remaining sour cream and salt.
- Stuff mixture (sideways) into half of each potato skin; spoon russet potato filling into other half.
- Place on a baking sheet.
- Bake at 350° for 15 to 20 minutes.

Serves 12

Classic Fried Green Tomatoes

4-6 green tomatoes
   Salt and pepper
   Cornmeal to dust
   Bacon grease or vegetable oil

- Slice tomatoes into ¼ to ½ inch slices. Salt and pepper to taste.
- Dip in cornmeal; fry in hot grease or oil about 3 minutes or until golden on bottom. Gently turn and fry the other side.

Serves 4 to 6

Green Beans Amandine

1   **pound fresh or frozen green beans, whole**
½   **cup water**
¼   **cup almonds, slivered**
2   **tablespoons butter**
1   **teaspoon lemon juice**
    Salt to taste

- In a saucepan, bring beans and water to a boil; reduce heat to medium. Cover and cook for 10 to 15 minutes or until beans are crisp-tender; drain and set aside.
- In a large skillet, sauté almonds in butter over low heat.
- Stir in lemon juice and salt.
- Add beans and heat through.

Serves 6

Yes, Southerners really do eat fried green tomatoes; and they eat fried red tomatoes too. If you haven't tried them, you're in for a treat! Tomatoes are native to Mexico and Central America; it's not clear how tomatoes came to the U.S. There is a folk legend that they were introduced by African slaves who came to North America by way of the Caribbean, and some historians believe that the Portuguese introduced tomatoes to the West Coast of Africa. There are plenty of ways to coat and fry your tomatoes – bread crumbs, cracker crumbs, cornmeal, or flour. Some people dip them in beaten eggs before dredging and some just dredge then fry. Salt and pepper them first and use bacon grease for the best results. They can be done in vegetable oil, they just won't have quite the same "Southern" flavor.

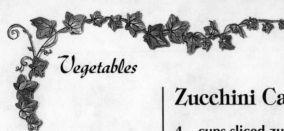

Zucchini Casserole Imperial

4   cups sliced zucchini
2   eggs, beaten
1   cup mayonnaise or salad dressing
1   onion, diced
¼   cup chopped green pepper
1   cup Parmesan cheese
     Salt and pepper to taste
     Water
1   tablespoon butter or margarine, melted
½   cup dry bread crumbs

- Preheat oven to 350°.
- Cook zucchini in small amount of water; drain and place in a greased 2 quart baking dish.
- In small bowl, combine eggs, mayonnaise, onion, green pepper, cheese, salt, pepper and mix well.
- Pour egg mixture over zucchini and stir lightly to combine.
- Combine melted butter and bread crumbs; sprinkle over casserole.
- Bake 30 minutes or until tender.

Serves 6 to 8

Desserts

Desserts

Apple Cobbler Cake

Cake

1½ cups salad or vegetable oil
2 cups sugar
3 eggs
2 teaspoons vanilla flavoring
3 cups plain flour
½ teaspoon salt
1 teaspoon soda
1 cup chopped pecans
3 cups peeled and chopped apples
   Topping (recipe follows)

- Preheat oven to 350°.
- Blend together cooking oil, sugar, eggs and vanilla flavoring.
- Sift together flour, soda and salt.
- Mix gradually with above blended ingredients.
- Fold in pecans and apples.
- Pour into well greased and floured tube pan.
- Bake 1 hour.

Topping

1 cup brown sugar
1 stick butter
¼ cup milk

- Boil brown sugar, butter and milk together for 3 minutes.
- Pour over hot cake.
- Let stand 1 hour before removing from pan.

Serves 16 to 20

Saving the best for last is a phrase that best describes dessert. While some people are vegetarians; others can't do without a perfectly cooked steak; dessert is the most anticipated course of the meal. Southerners take their dessert very seriously. As you page through this cookbook, take notice of the many wonderful recipes that folks have shared with us. Dessert may not be one of healthiest habits, but it's certainly one of the most pleasurable.

Best Ever Chocolate Cake

"God surely blessed us by sending hospice at this very hard time in our lives. Thank you from the bottom of our hearts for all the love, wonderful care, kindness and tenderness you extended to us during Mom's illness and her death. She also loved you."

Cake

2   **sticks margarine**
1   **cup cola-flavored carbonated drink**
3   **tablespoons cocoa**
2   **cups plain flour**
2   **cups sugar**
2   **eggs**
½   **cup buttermilk**
1   **teaspoon baking soda**
1   **teaspoon vanilla**
     Frosting (recipe follows)

• Preheat oven to 350°.
• Bring to a boil the margarine, cola-flavored drink and cocoa.
• Pour over the flour and sugar.
• Mix well by hand.
• Add eggs, buttermilk, baking soda and vanilla and mix well. Batter will be thin.
• Pour batter into 9 x 13 inch pan.
• Bake 35 to 40 minutes. (Do not overcook.)

Frosting

1   **stick margarine**
6   **tablespoons cola-flavored drink**
3   **tablespoons cocoa**
1   **box confectioners' sugar**
1   **teaspoon vanilla**

• Bring to a boil the margarine, cola-flavored drink and cocoa.
• Reduce heat to low and add confectioners' sugar, small amount at a time, beating it in well.
• After it is all stirred in, use hand mixer to smooth.
• Add vanilla.
• Pour over hot cake and let cool. Delicious!

Serves 20

Blueberry Cake

Cake

¼ **cup butter, softened**
¾ **cup sugar**
1 **egg**
2 **cups all-purpose flour**
2 **teaspoons baking powder**
  Pinch salt
½ **cup milk**
1¼ **cups blueberries, fresh or frozen**
1 **tablespoon flour**
  Crumb Topping (recipe follows)

- Preheat oven to 350°.
- Cream butter and sugar.
- Add egg and mix well.
- Mix in the flour, baking powder, salt and milk until well blended.
- Mix blueberries with 1 tablespoon flour.
- Stir berries into the batter.
- Pour into 8 inch square greased or sprayed pan.

Crumb Topping

½ **cup all-purpose flour**
¼ **cup butter**
½ **cup sugar**

- Blend flour, butter and sugar with a fork to make a coarse crumbly topping.
- Sprinkle on cake batter.
- Bake 55 minutes.

Serves 8 to 10

Along the banks of
the Savannah River,
Native Americans
some 4500 years ago
discovered that fire
could harden clay to a
stone-like consistency.
These unknown people
mixed Spanish moss or
palmetto fibers with the
clay to make the earliest
known pottery vessels
in North America. Most
typically formed where
storage jars from one-
half to 30 gallons,
commonly used for
pickling, salting meat,
storing lard, etc. They
also made pipes and
marbles for the simple
pleasures of life.

Italian Cream Cake

Our traditional Thanksgiving dinner cake.

Cake

1	stick butter
½	cup vegetable shortening
2	cups sugar
5	egg yolks
2	cups all-purpose flour, sifted
1	teaspoon soda
1	(3½ ounce) can coconut
1	cup buttermilk
1	teaspoon vanilla
1	cup chopped nuts
5	egg whites, well beaten
	Frosting (recipe follows)

- Preheat oven to 350°.
- In a large mixing bowl, cream butter, vegetable shortening and sugar together until fluffy.
- Add egg yolks, one at a time, beating well after each addition.
- Sift flour and soda together.
- Add alternately with milk and vanilla.
- Add chopped nuts and coconut and blend well.
- Beat egg whites and fold into mixture.
- Pour batter into 3 greased and floured 8 inch cake pans.
- Bake 25 minutes.
- Remove from oven and let cool.
- If you wish to make 4 layers, bake a little less time.

Frosting

1	(8 ounce) package cream cheese
1	box confectioners' sugar
½	stick butter, softened
1	teaspoon vanilla

Italian Cream Cake *continued*

- Mix cream cheese, sugar, butter and vanilla together until of spreading consistency.
- Spread between layers and on top of cake.

Serves 14 to 18

This cake is better after it sits several days.

Southern Comfort Cake

1 **pound golden raisins**
1 **cup Southern Comfort**
1 **cup butter**
2 **cups sugar**
6 **large eggs**
3½ **cups all-purpose flour**
2 **teaspoons baking powder**
1 **teaspoon salt**
1 **pound (1 quart) pecans, shelled and chopped**

- Soak raisins in bourbon overnight.
- Preheat oven to 325°.
- Grease and line bottom of 10 inch tube pan (may use 2 small tube pans).
- Cream butter and sugar. Gradually add one egg at a time, beating well after each egg.
- Sift flour, baking powder and salt. Add to egg mixture.
- Add raisins and pecans, mixing well.
- Bake for 1½ hours for tube pan, less time for smaller pans. Cool cake on rack.
- After cooling, wrap cake in cheesecloth soaked in Southern Comfort and place in airtight container. Will keep for several weeks.

Serves 16

Blueberry Pudding Cake

Cake

2	cups blueberries, fresh or frozen
1	teaspoon cinnamon
1	teaspoon lemon juice
1	cup all-purpose flour
¾	cup sugar
1	teaspoon baking powder
½	cup milk
3	tablespoons butter or margarine, melted
	Topping (recipe follows)

- Preheat oven to 350°.
- Toss blueberries with cinnamon and lemon juice.
- Place in a greased 8 inch square baking dish.
- Combine flour, sugar and baking powder in a bowl.
- Stir in milk and butter.
- Spoon berries over cake mixture.

Topping

¾	cup sugar
1	tablespoon cornstarch
1	cup boiling water

- Combine sugar and cornstarch.
- Sprinkle over batter.
- Slowly pour boiling water over all.
- Bake 45 minutes or until done.

Serves 8 to 10

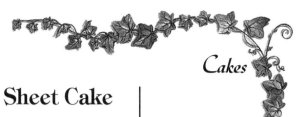

HospiceCare of the Piedmont Sheet Cake

Cake

2	**sticks margarine**
1	**cup water**
4	**tablespoons cocoa**
2	**cups sugar**
2	**cups all-purpose flour**
½	**teaspoon salt**
1	**teaspoon soda**
2	**eggs**
¾	**cup sour cream**
	Frosting (recipe follows)

- Preheat oven to 350°.
- In a small saucepan, bring margarine, water and cocoa to a boil.
- Combine sugar, flour, salt and soda.
- Pour boiled mixture over the sugar mixture.
- Add eggs and sour cream.
- Beat well and pour in a greased jelly-roll pan.
- Bake 20 minutes or until cake springs back.

Frosting

1	**stick margarine**
4	**tablespoons cocoa**
6	**tablespoons milk**
1	**box confectioners' sugar**
1	**cup walnuts, chopped**
1	**teaspoon vanilla**

- Mix margarine, cocoa, milk, sugar, walnuts and vanilla together until well blended.
- Frost while cake is hot.

Serves 18 to 20

As long as Southerners have been baking, cakes have been one of the most commonly served desserts. A covered dish supper in the South almost automatically means several cakes, beautifully displayed, at the buffet table.

A perfect cake results not from luck but from accurate measuring and proper mixing and baking. When baking cakes, make sure pans do not touch each other or the side of the oven. Stagger when placing on separate racks. Cool cakes thoroughly before storing. If you plan to freeze your cake, don't frost before freezing. Wrap in aluminum foil and then plastic wrap. Will keep up to 5 months this way.

Within the town limits of McCormick, gold was discovered in 1847 by William Dorn. The site of this strike was only a short distance from the present location of the McCormick Post Office. Dorn's Gold Mines, considered one of the largest strikes in South Carolina and one of the richest in the nation, produced over a million dollars worth of the precious metal. The settlement which grew up around the mines was known as Dorn's Gold Mines. A store and Dorn's Mines Post Office were located near the present location of the railroad depot.

The present town of McCormick is situated atop some 4½ miles of tunnels which led from the gold mines. After 1865, the mines were leased and operated by Major Maxwell and

Chocolate Peanut Butter Cake

Cake
2	sticks margarine
½	cup buttermilk
1	cup water
¼	cup cocoa
2	eggs, well beaten
2	cups sugar
2	cups all-purpose flour, unsifted
1	teaspoon baking soda
1	teaspoon vanilla
1	(12 ounce) jar peanut butter
1½	tablespoons peanut oil
	Frosting (recipe follows)

- Preheat oven to 350°.
- Mix in large saucepan over medium heat the margarine, buttermilk, water, cocoa and eggs.
- Stir until it bubbles freely.
- Add the sugar, flour, baking soda and vanilla.
- Mix well.
- Pour into a greased 9 x 13 inch pan.
- Bake at 25 minutes.
- When cool, mix peanut butter with 1½ tablespoons peanut oil.
- Spread this mixture over the cake.

Frosting
½	cup margarine
¼	cup cocoa
6	tablespoons buttermilk
1	box confectioners' sugar
1	teaspoon vanilla

- Bring margarine, cocoa and buttermilk to a good boil.
- Remove from heat and add confectioners' sugar and vanilla.
- Spread over peanut butter covered cake.

Serves 16 to 18

Gooey Butter Cake

Cake

3   **cups cake flour**
1¾ **cups sugar**
⅓   **cup dry milk**
2½ **teaspoons baking powder**
1   **teaspoon salt**
1   **cup butter plus 2 tablespoons butter, melted**
2   **eggs**
1½ **teaspoons vanilla**
     Topping (recipe follows)

- Preheat oven to 350°.
- Sift flour, sugar, dry milk, baking powder and salt in large bowl.
- Add butter, eggs, vanilla and beat.
- Spread into 11 x 16 inch jelly-roll pan.

Topping

1   **(8 ounce) package cream cheese**
2   **eggs**
1   **teaspoon vanilla**
1   **box confectioners' sugar**

- Beat together cream cheese, eggs and vanilla.
- Blend in confectioners' sugar.
- Carefully spread on cake batter.
- Bake at 30 minutes or until top is golden brown.

Serves 12 to 16

Dr. Vestree. Cyrus H. McCormick, of reaper fame, leased and later bought the mining property from "Billy" Dorn in the early 1870's, resulting in the name of the town and county. During the 1930's, when gold went up after the reevaluation of the dollar, the mines were reopened and operated. For nearly a century at one time or another, gold mining has been carried on within the town limits of McCormick.

"To the 'Guardian Angels' that guided me through the toughest part of my life; the loss of my mother. 'Thanks' is only part of the heartfelt gratitude these special wishes offer all of you today…for your caring attitudes, your helping and guiding hands, and a deep appreciation for sharing so much goodness from your hearts."

Chunky Apple Cake

3   cups all-purpose flour
2   cups sugar
1   cup salad oil
⅓   cup orange juice
1   teaspoon baking powder
1   teaspoon cinnamon
1   teaspoon vanilla
3   eggs
1½ cups nuts, chopped
1   large cooking apple (½ pound), chopped

- Preheat oven to 350°.
- In large bowl, with mixer at low speed, beat flour, sugar, oil, orange juice, baking powder, cinnamon, vanilla and eggs until blended. Beat 2 minutes at high speed.
- Fold in apple and nuts.
- Spoon into a greased and floured 10 inch tube pan.
- Bake 25 minutes.
- Cover loosely with foil and continue to bake for 1 hour.

Serves 10 to 12

Hot Fudge Pudding Cake

Base

¾   **cup sugar**
1   **cup all-purpose flour**
3   **tablespoons cocoa**
2   **teaspoons baking powder**
¼   **teaspoon salt**
½   **cup milk**
⅓   **cup butter or margarine, melted**
1½ **teaspoons vanilla**

- Preheat oven to 350°.
- In medium mixing bowl, combine the sugar, flour, cocoa, baking powder and salt.
- Blend in the milk, butter and vanilla.
- Beat until smooth.
- Pour batter into square 8 x 8 x 2 inch pan.

Second Layer

½   **cup sugar**
½   **cup firmly packed light brown sugar**
4   **tablespoons cocoa**

- In small bowl, combine sugar, brown sugar and cocoa.
- Sprinkle mixture evenly over the batter.

Third Layer
1½ **cups hot water**

- Pour hot water over the top - DO NOT STIR!
- Bake 40 minutes.
- Let stand 15 minutes.
- Spoon into dessert dishes, spooning sauce from the bottom of the pan over the top. Garnish with whipped cream or vanilla ice cream.

Serves 8 to 10

Chopped pecans (½ cup) can be added to the batter, if desired.

Amaretto Cheese Cake

Make a day or two ahead for the flavor to ripen.

Crust
1½ cups graham cracker crumbs
2   tablespoons sugar
1   teaspoon cinnamon
1   stick plus 2 tablespoons butter, melted
    Filling (recipe follows)
    Topping (recipe follows)

- Mix graham cracker crumbs, sugar, cinnamon and butter. Press into bottom of 8 or 9 inch springform pan and up the sides about ½ inch.

Filling
3   (8 ounce) packages cream cheese, softened
1   cup sugar
4   eggs
⅓   cup amaretto

- Preheat oven to 375°.
- Beat the cream cheese until it is fluffy.
- Gradually add sugar.
- Add eggs one at a time beating well after each egg.
- Stir in amaretto and pour into pan.
- Bake 45 to 50 minutes. Remove from oven and turn oven to 500°.

Topping
1   cup sour cream
1   tablespoon amaretto
2   tablespoons sugar

- Mix sour cream, amaretto and sugar and pour over cake.
- Put in the oven for 5 minutes at 500°.
- Let cake cool to room temperature and then refrigerate for 24 to 48 hours to ripen.

Amaretto Cheese Cake *continued*

Garnish

½   **cup roasted almonds, optional**
1   **tablespoon grated chocolate, optional**

- Decorate cake with almonds and chocolate.

Serves 16

Grandma's Nut Cake

½   **cup butter or margarine**
1½ **cups sugar**
3   **eggs, slightly beaten**
2½ **cups flour**
1½ **teaspoons baking powder**
½   **cup milk**
1   **cup chopped pecans, walnuts or hickory nuts**

- Preheat oven to 350°.
- Cream butter or margarine and sugar.
- Add slightly beaten eggs and mix well.
- Stir flour and baking powder together and add ½ to the mixture.
- Mix well.
- Stir in milk.
- Add remaining flour and baking powder and nuts.
- Mix well. Batter will be firm.
- Pour into greased 9 x 13 inch pan or 2 (8 inch) cake pans.
- Bake 30 to 40 minutes or until toothpick stuck in center comes out clean.

Serves 12 to 15

Pineapple Pound Cake

The name pound cake is derived from the original recipe - a pound of butter, a pound of sugar, a pound of flour and a pound of eggs. Pound cake is a versatile dessert: it can be served plain or toasted; top it with fruit or just a fruit sauce; or you can try out one of your favorite frosting recipes.

Cake

½ cup shortening
1 cup butter
2¾ cups sugar
6 eggs
3 cups all-purpose flour
1 teaspoon baking powder
1 teaspoon vanilla
¼ cup milk
¾ cup crushed pineapple, undrained
 Pineapple Glaze (recipe follows)

- Cream shortening, butter and sugar together until light and fluffy.
- Add eggs, one at a time, beating well after each addition.
- Sift together flour, baking powder.
- Add alternately to creamed mixture with vanilla and milk.
- Beat well after each addition.
- Stir in crushed pineapple.
- Pour batter into a well greased and floured tube pan.
- Place in a cold oven.
- Bake at 325° for 1 hour and 15 minutes.
- Cool 10 to 15 minutes in pan.
- Invert cake onto serving plate and drizzle pineapple glaze on top and sides.

Pineapple Glaze

¼ cup butter or margarine, melted
1½ cups confectioners' sugar
1 cup crushed pineapple, drained

- Combine butter and confectioners' sugar, mixing until smooth.
- Stir in pineapple.

Serves 16 to 18

Black Walnut Pound Cake

3	**sticks margarine**
1	**box confectioners' sugar**
5	**eggs**
½	**cup water, if necessary for mixing**
2	**cups all-purpose flour**
1	**teaspoon vanilla**
1	**cup black walnuts, finely chopped**

- Preheat oven to 325°.
- In a large mixing bowl, cream butter and sugar together until light and fluffy.
- Add eggs, one at a time, beating well after each addition.
- Add flour gradually and the water, if necessary.
- Add walnuts to batter and mix.
- Add vanilla.
- Pour into greased Bundt pan.
- Bake 1½ hours.

Serves 14 to 18

Very good with chocolate or vanilla frosting.

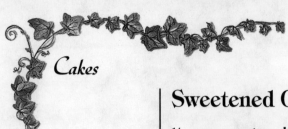

Sweetened Condensed Milk Pound Cake

½   cup sweetened condensed milk
4   sticks butter
     Pinch salt
1   teaspoon vanilla
3   cups sugar
8   eggs
3½ cups cake flour, sifted

- Have everything at room temperature.
- Mix sweetened condensed milk, butter, salt, vanilla and sugar together well.
- Add eggs, one at a time, beating well after each addition.
- Add flour.
- Start cake in cold oven. Bake at 300° for 1½ hours.

Serves 10 to 12

Milk Chocolate Pound Cake

4   bars milk chocolate candy
1   box yellow cake mix
1   (3.4 ounce) box instant vanilla pudding
1   cup sour cream
½   cup vegetable oil
4   eggs
1   box confectioners' sugar

- Preheat oven to 350°.
- Break chocolate candy into 1 inch size or process to "grated" size.
- Reserve in refrigerator.
- Mix cake mix, pudding, sour cream, oil and eggs until thoroughly mixed.
- Add chocolate pieces.
- Pour into a 10 inch greased and floured tube pan.
- Bake 55 minutes.
- Dust top of cake with sifted confectioners' sugar.

Serves 12 to 18

Even though a cake made from scratch is usually better tasting, keep a couple packages of commercial cake mix on hand. If you are short on time, this may be the answer to a good dessert by just adding a few extras. In fact, after the many compliments you will win with these cakes, you may find yourself baking with mixes even when you have plenty of time.

Blackberry Pound Cake

1   box yellow cake mix with pudding
1   cup oil
4   eggs
1   cup blackberry wine
1   small box blackberry jello

- Mix all above ingredients together well.
- Pour into a greased and floured pound cake pan.
- Bake according to time and temperature on cake mix box.

Serves 10 to 12

Earthquake Cake

1   box German chocolate cake mix
1½ cups water
⅓   cup oil
3   eggs
1   cup chopped nuts
1   cup coconut
1   stick margarine, melted
1   (8 ounce) package cream cheese
1   box 4X confectioners' sugar

* Preheat oven to 350°.
* Mix cake mix, water, oil and eggs.
* For crust, sprinkle nuts and coconut on bottom 9 x 13 inch pan.
* Pour cake mixture over pecans and coconut.
* Mix margarine, cream cheese and 4X sugar together.
* Carefully spread this mixture on top of cake mixture.
* Do not stir.
* Bake 45 minutes.

Serves 16 to 18

Chocolate Peppermint Sensation Cake

1   **package chocolate cake mix**
1   **(4 serving) package instant chocolate fudge pudding mix**
1   **(8 ounce) carton sour cream**
½   **cup cooking oil**
½   **cup strong brewed coffee or rum or water**
4   **eggs**
3   **teaspoons peppermint flavoring**
1   **(12 ounce) package semi-sweet chocolate chips**

- Preheat oven to 350°.
- Grease and flour 10 inch fluted tube pan.
- Combine cake mix, pudding, sour cream, cooking oil, coffee, rum or water, eggs and peppermint flavoring.
- Beat until blended for 4 minutes.
- Stir in chocolate chips.
- Pour into prepared pan.
- Bake 50 to 60 minutes.
- Let cool 10 minutes and remove from pan.

Serves 16 to 20

"…to thank your wonderful staff for the care they provided my mother. We could never have granted Mom's last request of dying a peaceful death at home without the assistance from your organization. I will always be grateful for the loving care they provided to Mom, but also to my sister, brother and myself. I always knew this community was so very fortunate to have hospice, but until I personally experienced this myself, I didn't realize we couldn't do without such a great and much needed program."

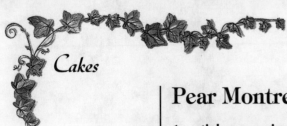

Pear Montreat Cake

1   stick margarine, melted
1   package yellow cake mix
1   egg, beaten
6   pear halves, canned
1   (4 ounce) carton sour cream
1   (8 ounce) package cream cheese, softened
1   teaspoon vanilla
2   large eggs

- Preheat oven to 325°.
- Combine melted margarine, cake mix and beaten egg in a bowl and mix well.
- Pat in the bottom of a 9 x 13 inch pan.
- Place pear halves on top of cake mixture.
- In a separate bowl, mix sour cream, softened cream cheese, vanilla and eggs.
- Beat together 5 to 6 minutes.
- Pour on top of cake mixture with pears.
- Bake 50 minutes.

Serves 8 to 10

Pecan Pie Cake

Cake

1 **package yellow cake mix**
1 **stick margarine**
1 **egg**
Topping (recipe follows)

- Preheat oven to 325°.
- Mix cake mix, butter and egg together.
- Set aside ⅔ cup of mixture.
- Spread remaining mixture in 8 inch square pan.
- Bake 15 minutes.
- Cool 10 minutes.

Topping

⅔ **cup batter from cake**
1½ **cups light corn syrup**
½ **cup dark brown sugar**
3 **eggs**
1 **teaspoon vanilla**
2 **cups pecans, chopped and toasted**

- In the remaining ⅔ cup batter, add corn syrup, brown sugar, eggs and vanilla. Fold in nuts.
- Pour over warm cake layer.
- Continue baking at 325° 40 to 45 minutes.

Serves 6 to 8

"We love you and God Bless each and everyone of you."

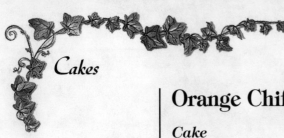

Orange Chiffon Cake

Cake

5   egg whites
½   teaspoon cream of tartar
1   package yellow cake mix
3   egg yolks
¾   cup orange juice
½   cup vegetable oil
1   teaspoon orange zest
    Glaze (recipe follows)

- Preheat oven to 325°.
- Beat egg whites, add cream of tartar and beat until stiff.
- In a separate bowl, combine cake mix, egg yolks, orange juice, oil and orange zest.
- Fold in egg whites.
- Pour in non-stick round tube cake pan.
- Bake 45 to 50 minutes.
- Cool cake 1 hour.

Glaze

1   cup confectioners' sugar
3   teaspoons orange juice

- Blend confectioners' sugar and orange juice together until well blended.
- Pour glaze over cake.

Serves 12 to 16

 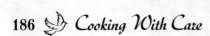

The Best Pineapple Cake

Cake
1   box yellow cake mix
1   (3.4 ounce) package lemon instant pudding
¾   cup salad or vegetable oil
4   eggs
10 ounces lemon-lime carbonated drink
     Frosting (recipe follows)

- Preheat oven to 325°.
- Mix the cake mix, pudding, oil, eggs and lemon-lime carbonated drink together well.
- Bake in a nonstick 9 x 13 inch sheet pan for 30 minutes.

Frosting
1½ cups sugar
2   tablespoons all-purpose flour
2   beaten eggs
1   (8 ounce) can crushed pineapple
1   (3.5 ounce) can coconut

- Mix sugar and flour.
- Combine beaten eggs and pineapple in saucepan and cook until thick, stirring often.
- Let cool.
- Add coconut.
- Stir and spread over cake.

Serves 8 to 10

Busy Day Cheese Cake

1   box yellow cake mix
2   sticks butter or margarine
1   can prepared frosting (any flavor-chocolate, lemon or vanilla)
1   (8 ounce) carton vanilla yogurt
2   (8 ounce) packages cream cheese
3   well beaten eggs

- Preheat oven to 325°.
- Crumble cake mix and butter or margarine together until well blended.
- Press into deep pie dish or large glass casserole, reserving ½ cup.
- Mix together frosting, yogurt, cream cheese and eggs.
- Pour into cake mix crust.
- Sprinkle the top with the reserved ½ cup crumbs.
- Bake at 325° for 70 minutes and 350° for 60 minutes.

Serves 8 to 10

You may substitute any flavor cake mix.

Black Russian Cake

Cake

1	**(18.5-ounce) package yellow cake mix**
1	**(3-ounce) package instant chocolate pudding**
4	**eggs**
1	**cup vegetable oil**
¾	**cup water**
½	**cup Kahlúa liqueur**
¼	**cup vodka**
½	**cup chopped pecans**
	Glaze (recipe follows)

- Preheat oven to 350°.
- Combine cake mix, pudding, eggs, oil, water, Kahlúa and vodka and mix well for 2 minutes. Stir in pecans.
- Pour into a greased and floured 10 inch tube pan.
- Bake 55 to 60 minutes.

Glaze

1	**cup confectioners' sugar**
2	**tablespoons Kahlúa**

- Mix confectioners' sugar and Kahlúa to make glaze. Drizzle over cake.

Serves 12 to 14

"My days are better days when they come to give me a bath. I feel better then."

Amaretto Angel Cake

1   ready to eat angel food cake (loaf or tube type)
12 tablespoons amaretto (divided)
½   gallon ice cream (any flavor), softened
    Frosting (recipe follows)

- Split cake into 3 horizontal sections.
- Place first section on cake plate. Drizzle with 3 tablespoons amaretto. Cover with 2 inches of ice cream.
- Place second section of cake on top of ice cream layer. Drizzle with 3 tablespoons amaretto. Cover with 2 inches of ice cream.
- Place third section of cake on top of layer 2. Drizzle with 3 tablespoons of amaretto.

3   tablespoons amaretto
1   (16 ounce) container whipped topping

- Fold 3 tablespoons of amaretto into whipped topping.
- Frost cake with mixture. Freeze.

Serves 12 to 14

Amaretto keeps cake from freezing hard, so you can remove it from freezer and serve immediately.

Butterscotch (Boiled) Cookies

1   cup brown sugar
1   cup white sugar
½   cup milk
1   stick margarine
3   cups quick oats
1   teaspoon vanilla
1   cup chopped nuts (optional)

- Preheat oven to 350°.
- Combine brown sugar, white sugar, milk and margarine in large saucepan.
- Put on stove and boil for 2 minutes.
- Remove from heat and fold in oats, vanilla and nuts.
- Drop from teaspoon onto a greased cookie sheet.
- Bake about 8 to 10 minutes or until done.

2 dozen cookies

Lemon Snowdrops

1   cup butter
½   cup confectioners' sugar
1   teaspoon lemon extract
2   cups all-purpose flour
¼   teaspoon salt
    Lemon curd

- Prepare pie filling according to package directions. Set aside.
- Preheat oven to 350°.
- In a mixing bowl, cream butter and sugar; add extract.
- Sift together flour and salt; add to creamed mixture and mix well.
- Roll even teaspoonful into balls. Place 1 inch apart on ungreased cookie sheets; flatten slightly.
- Bake 8 to 10 minutes. Let cool. Sprinkle with confectioners' sugar. Place dollop of prepared lemon curd on top of each cookie.

4 to 5 dozen cookies

Cookies are a bite size confection that brings back many a childhood memory. Coming home from school and smelling cookies baking is a very fond memory for many of us. It's such a challenge to keep a cookie jar filled - it isn't difficult to make cookies, it's just difficult to keep them from disappearing.

TIPS: Always bake cookies in a preheated oven unless specified otherwise. Grease cookie sheets only if directed. For best results, bake only one pan of cookies at a time. Personal preference in cookies vary, so when testing for doneness take into consideration whether you like soft, chewy cookies or crisp ones. Leaving them in the oven 1 to 2 minutes longer make them crispier. Let cookies cool completely before storing.

Cheese Cake Bars

Bars
2 **packages crescent rolls**
2 **(8 ounce) packages cream cheese**
1 **cup sugar**
1 **egg yolk - save egg white**
1 **teaspoon vanilla**
Topping (recipe follows)

- Preheat oven to 350°.
- Place one package crescent rolls in greased 9 x 13 inch dark glass or non-stick pan.
- Gently press seams together to make one flat base.
- Mix cream cheese, sugar, egg yolk and vanilla together well.
- Spread over base.
- Unfold second can of crescent rolls and place over the mixture.
- Gently press seams together.

Topping
1 **egg white**
1 **teaspoon cinnamon**
½ **cup sugar**
½ **chopped nuts, optional**

- Beat egg white with a fork.
- Spread over the top layer of crescent rolls.
- Mix cinnamon and sugar and sprinkle over egg white.
- Top with nuts, if desired.
- Bake 30 minutes.
- After cooling, store in refrigerator.

24 to 36 small bars

Best served at room temperature.

Lemon Crispies

1   (18½ ounce) package lemon cake mix with pudding
1   egg
2   cups frozen whipped topping, thawed
1   teaspoon lemon zest
1   package confectioners' sugar

- Preheat oven 350°.
- Blend cake mix, egg, thawed topping, and lemon zest well.
- Dip rounded teaspoonfuls in powdered sugar to form balls.
- Place balls 1½ inches apart on ungreased cookie sheet.
- Bake 10 to 12 minutes.
- Remove immediately and cool on wire racks.

60 cookies

Can't Eat Just One Cookies

½   cup margarine
2   cups brown sugar
3   eggs, well beaten
2   cups all-purpose flour
1   teaspoon vanilla
½   cup nuts, chopped
1   small bottle maraschino cherries, chopped
48 miniature marshmallows
    Confectioners' sugar

- Preheat oven 350°.
- Cream margarine and sugar.
- Add eggs, flour and vanilla and mix well.
- Add nuts, cherries and marshmallows.
- Place in greased 8 x 10 inch pan.
- Bake 40 minutes.
- Cool slightly and cut into squares.
- Roll in confectioners' sugar.

16 to 20 cookies

Orange Sugar Cookies

Cookies
¼ cup shortening
1 cup sugar
2 eggs, beaten
2 teaspoons orange zest
3½ cups all-purpose flour, sifted
3 teaspoons baking powder
½ teaspoon salt
½ teaspoon vanilla
½ cup milk
   Cream Frosting (recipe follows)

- Preheat oven to 375°.
- Cream shortening and sugar.
- Beat eggs and orange zest into mixture.
- Sift together flour, baking powder and salt.
- Add ½ of dry ingredients to creamed mixture and mix well.
- Add vanilla, milk and remaining dry ingredients mixing well.
- Chill well.
- Roll ¼-inch thick on lightly floured board or pastry cloth.
- Cut into shapes with cookie cutters.
- Bake 8 to 10 minutes on ungreased cookie sheet.

Butter Cream Frosting
½ cup butter or margarine
2 cups confectioners' sugar, sifted
1 teaspoon vanilla
1 tablespoon cream

- Cream butter or margarine and sugar together well.
- Add vanilla and cream and stir until mixture is thick and creamy.
- If a thicker mixture is desired, add additional confectioners' sugar.

6 dozen cookies

Peachy Keen Cookies

½   **cup butter**
1   **cup sugar**
1   **egg**
2   **cups all-purpose flour**
½   **teaspoon baking soda**
¼   **teaspoon nutmeg**
¼   **teaspoon cinnamon**
⅛   **teaspoon ginger**
⅛   **teaspoon ground cloves**
3   **ripe peaches, peeled, pitted and finely diced**

- Preheat oven to 375°.
- Cream butter and sugar in a bowl.
- Add egg and beat until light and fluffy.
- In another bowl, mix flour, baking soda, nutmeg, cinnamon, ginger and cloves.
- Stir flour mixture into egg mixture, a little at a time.
- Stir peaches into cookie mixture.
- Drop by teaspoonful onto non-stick cookie sheet.
- Bake 20 minutes until cookies are browned on top.
- Cool thoroughly on wire rack before storing.

4 dozen (2½) inch cookies

These are soft, cake-like cookies. If cookies become too soft on standing, put them into a warm 250 to 300° oven for a few minutes.

"Our social worker did a fine job; she was always available to assist us and made sure follow up was done."

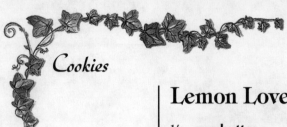

Lemon Love Notes

½ **cup butter**
1 **cup sifted all-purpose flour**
¼ **cup confectioners' sugar**
1 **cup sugar**
2 **tablespoons flour**
½ **teaspoon baking powder**
2 **eggs, beaten**
2 **tablespoons lemon juice**
2 **teaspoons lemon zest**

- Preheat oven to 350°.
- Mix butter, flour and confectioners' sugar.
- Press in ungreased 8 inch square pan.
- Bake 8 minutes or until golden brown.
- Cool in pan on rack.
- Combine sugar, 2 tablespoons flour and baking powder.
- Add eggs, lemon juice and zest.
- Mix well. Pour evenly over baked, cooled mixture in pan.
- Bake 25 minutes (top puffs up in baking and falls in cooling).
- Cool in pan on oven rack.
- Cut 2 inch squares.
- Sprinkle with confectioners' sugar.

16 squares

No-Cook Candy Ice Cream

2   pints heavy cream
1½ cups sugar
1   tablespoon vanilla
2   cups milk
1   cup crushed Turtles or Snickers bars
    (Freeze candy before crushing.)

- In a large mixing bowl, combine cream, sugar, vanilla, milk and crushed candy.
- Mix until well blended.
- Put mixture into a 4 or 5 quart ice cream freezer.
- Freeze.

Serves 10 to 12

"A special thanks to the chaplain. He was wonderful and the special Christmas caroling was so beautiful. No, you do not leave us alone; God's inner love has been expressed through you."

Chocolate Ice Cream

1   (14 ounce) can sweetened condensed milk
⅓   cup water
1   (8 ounce) carton frozen whipped topping
1   gallon chocolate milk

- Mix sweetened condensed milk and water in ice cream churn.
- Add whipped topping and chocolate milk.
- Mix until whipped topping is thoroughly mixed in.
- Churn until electric churn stops (approximately 30 to 45 minutes).
- Let set 10 to 15 minutes prior to serving.

Serves 10 to 12

No sound is more welcome on a hot summer day than the cranking of the ice cream freezer. At a family gathering, this activity brings everyone, both young and old alike, to share the fun and excitement. The most difficult part of this process is keeping everyone from lifting the lid. Don't skimp on the ice and salt; they're essential for proper freezing.

Dazzle your family and friends with colorful ice cream molds and flavors. There are molds designed specifically for ice cream, but any mold will work. Metal molds are the best because the metal freezes the ice cream faster. Oil or line mold with plastic wrap. Let ice cream soften at room temperature a few minutes before unmolding. You can apply a warm cloth to the outside of the mold for a few minutes to speed up the process.

Orange Sherbet

1   (2 liter) bottle of orange soda
1   (14 ounce) can sweetened condensed milk

- Pour soda and milk in churn.
- Churn for about 45 minutes or until done.
- Let sit prior to serving.
- May add small can crushed pineapple if desired.

Serves 10 to 12

Fresh Peach Ice Cream

10-12 ripe peaches
1   pint light cream
½   pint whipping cream
1   pint milk
1   (13 ounce) can evaporated milk
2   cups sugar
½   teaspoon almond flavoring

- Peel and slice peaches.
- Mash one or two peaches to a soft mush.
- Puree remaining peaches in blender - should have about 1 quart of peaches in all.
- Add sugar, light cream, whipping cream, milk, evaporated milk, sugar and almond flavoring.
- Stir well to dissolve sugar.
- Pour in a 1 gallon churn.
- Freeze.

1 gallon

Brown Sugar Brownies

1 **cup brown sugar**
½ **cup butter, melted**
1 **egg, well beaten**
1 **cup self-rising flour**
1 **teaspoon vanilla**
1 **cup nuts, chopped**

- Preheat oven to 350°.
- Cream brown sugar and butter together.
- Add the beaten egg.
- Add flour to the above mixture and stir until well blended.
- Add vanilla and nuts.
- Pour into greased 8 x 8 inch baking dish.
- Bake for 20 to 25 minutes.

Serves 8

Raspberry Sauce

2 **(10 ounce) packages frozen raspberries**
½ **cup sugar**
1 **teaspoon cornstarch**
2 **tablespoons lemon juice, freshly squeezed**

- Thaw raspberries and puree in blender.
- Strain seeds.
- Add sugar and bring to a boil in saucepan.
- Add cornstarch dissolved in lemon juice.
- Cook until slightly thickened.
- Cool and chill.
- Serve over pistachio ice cream or almond flavored ice cream.
- Good to serve during peach season.

Serves 8 to 10

Quick & Elegant Dessert (Adults Only)

½-¾ cup Kahlúa or amaretto, divided
1   (12 pack) box ice cream sandwiches
1   cup nuts, chopped - walnuts, pecans or almonds, divided
1   (8 ounce) carton frozen whipped topping

- Drizzle Kahlúa or amaretto in bottom of 9 x 13 inch baking dish.
- Arrange ice cream sandwiches to fill bottom of dish.
- Poke holes in sandwiches with fork or toothpick.
- Sprinkle ½ of the nuts over this.
- Drizzle with remaining Kahlúa or amaretto.
- Cover with whipped topping.
- Sprinkle with remaining nuts.
- Freeze 2 to 3 hours.
- Let soften 20 to 30 minutes before serving.

Serves 8 to 10

Apple Walnut Chips

2   cans apple pie filling
1   teaspoon cinnamon
1   teaspoon lemon juice
1   package yellow cake mix
1   cup walnuts or pecans, chopped
2   sticks margarine

- Preheat oven to 350°.
- Spoon apple pie filling into a non-stick 8 x 8 inch square pan.
- Sprinkle cinnamon and lemon juice over filling.
- Pour dry cake mix evenly over this mixture.
- Drizzle melted margarine over dry cake mix. (DO NOT STIR.)
- Sprinkle chopped nuts on top of the above.
- Bake for 55 minutes.

Serves 10 to 12

No Fail Fudge

4   cups sugar
2   sticks butter or margarine
1   cup milk
1¼ cups peanut butter
2   cups marshmallow cream
1   cup all-purpose flour
1   cup chopped nuts, optional

- Place sugar, margarine or butter and milk in heavy saucepan.
- Cook over low heat, stirring until sugar and margarine or butter melts.
- Continue cooking over medium heat, stirring often until mixture reaches soft ball stage (240°).
- Remove from heat.
- Add peanut butter and marshmallow cream, stirring until smooth.
- Add flour and stir quickly just until blended.
- Mix in nuts.
- Pour into greased 12 x 9 x 2 inch pan.
- Cool and cut into squares.

Serves 15 to 20

Lander University

This university has been providing educational and cultural opportunities since its founding in 1872. Lander is now a 4-year, coeducational, state-assisted university. Located in the heart of Greenwood, Lander serves as a hub for cultural enrichment in the western Piedmont area of South Carolina. Lander's varsity athletic teams have reaped honors at both district and national levels. The University's 130,000 square foot John Drummond Complex offers basketball fans the opportunity to watch the Senators play in the new 2,500-seat Finis Horne Arena.

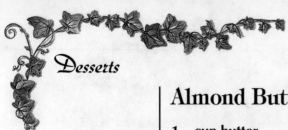

Almond Butter Crunch

1   cup butter
1   cup sugar
1½ cups sliced almonds
1   cup semi-sweet chocolate chips

- Melt butter in saucepan.
- Add sugar and almonds.
- Cook on medium heat until golden brown (about 10 minutes), stirring constantly.
- Pour into jelly-roll pan and press flat with spoons that have been chilled in the freezer.
- Sprinkle chocolate chips on top until they melt.
- Spread melted chips with a spatula.
- Put in refrigerator.
- Break into pieces when thoroughly chilled.

Many pieces

Layered Lemon Dessert

First Layer

1   **cup cold butter or margarine**
2   **cups all-purpose flour**
1   **cup finely chopped pecans**

- Preheat oven to 350°.
- In a bowl, cut butter into flour until mixture resembles coarse crumbs; stir in pecans. Press into an ungreased 9 x 13 inch baking pan.
- Bake for 15 minutes or until lightly browned. Cool on wire rack.

Second Layer

2   **(8 ounce) packages cream cheese, softened**
1   **cup confectioners' sugar**
1   **cup whipping cream, whipped**

- In a medium mixing bowl, combine cream cheese and sugar; mix well. Fold in whipped cream; spread over cooled crust.

Third Layer

2   **(3.25 ounce) packages lemon pudding - do not use instant**
1   **cup sugar**
4½ **cups cold water, divided**
4   **egg yolks**

- In a medium pan, combine pudding mix, sugar, 1 cup water and egg yolks until smooth. Stir in the remaining water. Bring to a boil over medium heat; cool. Spread over cream cheese layer.

Top Layer

2   **cups whipping cream**
2   **tablespoons sugar**
1   **teaspoon vanilla extract**

- In a small mixing bowl, beat cream, sugar and vanilla until stiff peaks form; spread over lemon layer. Refrigerate until serving.

Serves 15

"We were very satisfied with our social worker. She was always there when we needed her. Thank you so much."

Coffee & Dessert Pumpkin Roll

Pumpkin Roll

3	**eggs**
1	**cup sugar**
⅓	**cup pumpkin**
1	**teaspoon lemon juice**
2	**teaspoons cinnamon**
1	**teaspoon ginger**
½	**teaspoon nutmeg**
¾	**cup all-purpose flour**
¼	**cup nuts, pecans or walnuts**

- Preheat oven to 375°.
- Beat eggs for 5 minutes.
- Add sugar, pumpkin, lemon juice, cinnamon, ginger, nutmeg and flour.
- Mix well
- Spread on 15 x 10 inch cookie sheet.
- Top with nuts, broken in pieces.
- Bake for 15 minutes.
- Place on floured tea towel.
- Sprinkle with powdered sugar.
- Roll up and chill.

Filling

1	**cup powdered sugar**
1	**(8 ounce) package cream cheese**
4	**tablespoons butter**
½	**teaspoon milk**

- Blend sugar, cream cheese, butter and milk together well.
- Unroll pumpkin roll and spread filling on top.
- Roll again and chill.

Serves 10 to 12

Gatewood Club's Bread Pudding with Hard Whiskey Sauce

Bread Pudding

1   **loaf French bread**
1   **quart heavy cream**
3   **eggs**
1½ **cups sugar**
2   **tablespoons vanilla extract**
1   **teaspoon nutmeg**
1   **teaspoon allspice**
1   **tablespoon cinnamon**
1   **cup raisins**
3   **tablespoons butter or margarine**

- Preheat oven to 350°.
- Break bread into small pieces in a bowl.
- Add heavy cream to bread and soak.
- Use hands to crush bread and mix well
- Add eggs, sugar, vanilla extract, nutmeg, allspice, cinnamon and raisins and stir well.
- Grease a thick pan with butter
- Pour in pudding.
- Bake at 350° for 45 minutes or until very firm.
- Place on individual dessert plates.
- When ready to serve, add sauce and heat under broiler.

Hard Whiskey Sauce

1   **cup sugar**
1   **stick margarine**
1   **egg, beaten**
1-2 ounces whiskey, or to taste

- Put sugar and butter in double boiler and cook until well dissolved.
- Add egg and whip rapidly so egg doesn't curdle.
- Allow to cool.
- Add whiskey to taste.

"I want you to know how very much I appreciate everything you have done and are doing for us. Meeting you just once was enough for us. We liked you very much and wanted you to visit and pray with us."

Serves 8 to 10

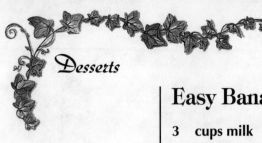

Southerners are
particular about their
Banana Pudding, but
we think this quick
version will please even
the most discriminating
palate.

Easy Banana Pudding

3   cups milk
1   (8 ounce) package cream cheese
1   (14 ounce) can sweetened condensed milk
1   large box instant vanilla pudding
5   bananas, sliced
1   large carton frozen whipped topping, thawed, divided
1   large box vanilla wafers

• In a large mixing bowl, mix, milk, cream cheese, condensed milk, pudding and ½ cup whipped topping together until thick.
• In a 9 x 13 inch dish, layer wafers, pudding mixture and bananas.
• Top with remaining whipped topping.
• Garnish with a few crushed vanilla wafers.
• Refrigerate until set.

Serves 8 to 10

Twinkies Dessert

10 Twinkies, sliced in half
3-4 bananas, sliced
1   (5½ ounce) package vanilla instant pudding
1   (20 ounce) can crushed pineapple, drained
1   (8 ounce) carton frozen whipped topping
    Maraschino cherries to garnish

• Place halve of Twinkies, cream side up in a square pan.
• Layer bananas over Twinkies.
• Mix pudding according to package directions.
• Pour over bananas.
• Spread pineapple over bananas.
• Spread thawed frozen whipped topping over bananas.
• Add maraschino cherries as garnish.
• Chill 2 hours.

Serves 6 to 8

Gooey Peach Pie

3	large very ripe peaches, sliced
1	stick unsalted butter, melted
1	cup sugar
1	teaspoon almond flavoring
1	egg, slightly beaten
3	tablespoons all-purpose flour
1	pie crust

- Preheat oven to 350°.
- Place peaches in pie crust.
- Mix melted unsalted butter, sugar, flavoring, egg and flour together thoroughly and pour over peaches.
- Bake until slightly browned and bubbly - about 1 hour and 15 minutes.
- Cool and serve.

Serves 6

The South is probably better known for its pies and pastries than any other dessert. Whether you make your own pie crust or use a store bought crust, pie is always a good choice for dessert. Serving fruit pies with a scoop of ice cream is a long time Southern custom. If you have a large crowd, scoop the ice cream balls a day ahead of time, and freeze them on a baking sheet.

There's almost an endless choice of pie varieties; fruit pies, cream pies, custard pies, vegetable and nut pies to name some. And we must never forget about the juicy fruit cobblers - a category to themselves.

Chocolate Pie

1½	cups sugar
3½	tablespoons cocoa
1	stick margarine, melted
1	(5 ounce) can evaporated milk
2	eggs, beaten
1	tablespoon vanilla
1	cup chopped nuts
1	(9 inch) deep dish pie crust

- Preheat oven to 325°.
- Mix all ingredients together well in order given above. Pour into a 9-inch deep dish pie crust.
- Bake 55 minutes.

Serves 6 to 8

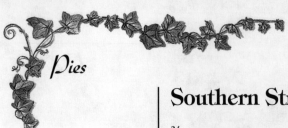

Southern Strawberry Pie

¾ **cup sugar**
2 **tablespoons cornstarch**
2 **tablespoons light corn syrup**
1 **cup water**
3 **tablespoons strawberry jello**
1 **(9 inch) baked pie shell**
1 **quart fresh strawberries, cleaned and hulled**
   whipped topping or cream

- Combine sugar, cornstarch, corn syrup and water in a saucepan.
- Bring to a boil.
- Cook, stirring constantly until clear and thickened.
- Add jello, stirring until dissolved. Refrigerate until cooled.
- Place strawberries in pie shell.
- Pour gelatin mixture over strawberries.
- Chill until firm.
- Top with whipped topping or cream.

Serves 6 to 8

Coconut-Caramel Pie

¼ **cup butter**
1 **(7 ounce) package flaked coconut**
½ **cup chopped pecans**
1 **(8 ounce) package cream cheese, softened**
1 **(14 ounce) can sweetened condensed milk**
1 **(12 ounce) container frozen whipped topping, thawed**
2 **graham cracker pie shells**
1 **(12 ounce) jar caramel ice cream topping**

- Melt butter in large skillet.
- Add coconut and pecans.
- Cook until golden brown, stirring often. Set aside.
- Combine cream cheese and condensed milk and beat until smooth.
- Fold in whipped topping.
- Layer ¼ cream mixture in each pie shell.
- Drizzle ¼ caramel ice cream topping on each pie.
- Sprinkle ¼ coconut mix and pecan mixture on each.
- Repeat layers to use all of ingredients.
- Cover and freeze.
- Treat as if ice cream pie when serving.

Serves 8 per pie

"Our social worker was great; so supportive, really caring and concerned."

Pineapple Coconut Pie

¼ **pound margarine**
2 **cups sugar**
4 **eggs, well beaten**
½ **(20 ounce) can crushed pineapple**
1 **(3½ ounce) can flaked coconut**
2 **shallow pastry shells**

- Preheat oven to 350°.
- Melt margarine and sugar, cooking until sugar dissolved.
- Add beaten eggs, pineapple and coconut.
- Pour into the pastry shells.
- Bake about 40 minutes.

Serves 12

Snicker Pie (Low-Fat)

½ **gallon fat-free frozen vanilla yogurt, softened**
1 **(6 ounce) package sugar-free instant chocolate pudding**
½ **cup crunchy peanut butter**
1 **(8 ounce) carton frozen whipped topping**

- Combine yogurt, pudding, peanut butter and whipped topping until mixed well.
- Pour into 2 (8-inch) pie pans sprayed with non-stick cooking spray.
- Freeze.

2 pies - Serves 8 per pie

Tropical Dream Pie

1   (16 ounce) can sour pitted cherries, drained - reserving juice
1   (20 ounce) can crushed pineapple, drained - reserving juice
⅔   cup sugar
¼   cup all-purpose flour
1   (3 ounce) package orange flavored gelatin
1   (3 ounce) package lemon gelatin
3   bananas
1   cup chopped pecans
2   (9 inch) baked pie shells, cooled
    Whipped topping, optional

- Combine juice from cherries and pineapple to make ½ cup.
- Combine sugar with flour.
- Add juice and cook until thick.
- Stir in the gelatins while liquid is hot and until gelatins are thoroughly dissolved.
- Add cherries, pineapple, bananas and pecans.
- Pour into baked pie shells.
- Place in the refrigerator until congealed thoroughly.
- Serve with whipped cream on top, if desired.

Serves 12

"Thank you for taking the time to help with my husband's funeral. You are a very special person."

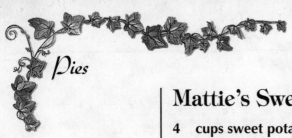

Mattie's Sweet Potato Pie

4   cups sweet potatoes (boiled in skin), peeled
2   sticks butter
2   cups sugar
1½ teaspoons vanilla extract
1¼ cups evaporated milk
3   eggs
1   baked pie shell
2   tablespoons butter, melted

The BEST SWEET POTATO PIE ever! A lady who cooked at Connie Maxwell Children's Home, Mattie, shared this recipe with me in 1977. I was very flattered that she shared it because it belonged to her grandmother.

- Preheat oven to 350°.
- In a large bowl, mash potatoes; add butter and let melt.
- Add sugar, vanilla, milk and eggs; beat this well.
- Bake until crust is brown and pie is a little brown on top (approximately 45 minutes to 1 hour).
- After about 30 minutes of baking time, remove pie from oven and brush the crust with melted butter. Return to oven to complete baking.

Serves 8

Fresh Peach Pie

1½ cups hot water
1½ cups sugar
     Dash salt
4   tablespoons cornstarch
4   tablespoons peach jello
3   cups sliced fresh peaches
1   baked pie shell

- Pour hot water over sugar, salt and cornstarch.
- Cook until thick, stirring continuously.
- Remove from heat.
- Add peach jello and mix well.
- Cool.
- Place peaches in baked pie shell.
- Pour jello mixture over peaches and chill.

Serves 6 to 8

Kids in the Kitchen

Kids in the Kitchen

Crispy Rice Kisses

3   **tablespoons butter or margarine**
10 **ounces marshmallow**
6   **cups crisp rice cereal**
      Non-stick cooking spray

- Melt butter in large sauce pan over low heat.
- Add marshmallows and stir until completely melted. Remove from heat.
- Mix in cereal until well coated.
- Coat the inside of a cone shaped funnel with cooking spray and pack with cereal mixture. Remove from funnel and wrap with aluminum foil to make a "kiss'. If you want a chocolate kiss, use chocolate flavored cereal.

Many kisses

Heart Shaped Crispy Rice - Spread half of the cereal mixture into a 9 x 9 inch square pan and half into a 9 inch round pan. Cut round pan in half. On a cake board, place the square mixture at an angle resembling a diamond shape. Place the two halves of the round mixture on the top two sides to form a heart shape. If you want to color the heart, place a few drops of food coloring into the melted marshmallows. Happy Valentines!

Mystic Punch

4   **(1 pint) bottles cranberry juice**
2½ **cups peach juice**
1   **cup fresh lime juice**
2   **cups orange juice**
      Sugar to taste
      Make ice cubes with raisins in them

- Combine cranberry juice, peach juice, lime juice, orange juice and sugar in a large punch bowl. Add the ice cubes with the "insects" in them.

3 quarts

Baked Apples with Night Crawlers

12 **large apples**
   Blackberry jam
4 **tablespoons butter**
12 **gummy worms**

- Preheat oven to 350°.
- Core apples from stem end to within ½ inch from bottom. Stuff each hole with 1 teaspoon jam and butter.
- Place on a cookie sheet and bake uncovered for 35 to 45 minutes.
- Remove apples; let stand for 15 minutes. Set each apple in a bowl and spoon syrup from baking pan around it. Insert a gummy worm with half its body protruding.

Gummy Worms & Bears

1 (4 ounce) box gelatin (with sugar), any flavor
7 envelopes unflavored gelatin
½ cup water

- Combine flavored gelatin, unflavored gelatin and water in saucepan; cook over low heat until melted. Once completely melted, pour into plastic candy molds and place in freezer for 5 minutes. When very firm, take out of molds.

Caramel Marshmallow Apples

1 **(14 ounce) package caramels**
1 **cup miniature marshmallows**
1 **tablespoon water**
6 **small apples**
6 **wooden popsicle sticks or skewers**
   Chopped peanuts, melted chocolate (optional)

- Line baking sheet with greased waxed paper; set aside.
- Combine caramels, marshmallows and water in medium saucepan. Cook over medium heat, stirring constantly, until caramels melt.
- Cool slightly. Rinse and dry apples.
- Insert stick into stem end of apple. Dip each apple in caramel mixture, coating apples. Place on baking sheet.
- Refrigerate until firm.
- For variety, roll apples in crushed peanuts or drizzle with melted chocolate.

Serves 6

Candied Apples

12 Red Delicious apples
12 wooden popsicle sticks or skewers
4½ cups white sugar
¾ cup light corn syrup
1 teaspoon red food coloring
1½ cups water
1 cup chopped peanuts

- Grease a large cookie sheet and set aside. Wash and dry apples thoroughly; insert a stick through stem end leaving about 2 inches sticking out.

- In saucepan over medium heat, combine sugar, corn syrup, food coloring and water. Cook, stirring constantly, until ingredients are dissolved and liquid boils. Set a candy thermometer in mixture and continue cooking, without stirring, until temperature reaches 290°, about 20 minutes.

- Meanwhile, place chopped peanuts in a shallow bowl. Remove syrup from heat and dip the apples, to coat evenly. You will have to work quickly. As you dip each apple, roll in peanuts to coat then place on cookie sheet.

- Let apples cool for at least an hour.

Serves 12

Chocolate Spiders

4 cups chocolate chips

- Melt chocolate chips in top of double boiler or microwave.
- Let stand until the water is cool.
- Place waxed paper on cookie sheet. Pour chocolate into a pastry bag or a plastic bag with a ⅛ inch tip or hole.
- Squeeze chocolate onto paper in the shape of spiders. If chocolate is runny it needs to cool longer. Chill the spider for about 10 minutes. When hard, peel off waxed paper. Store in refrigerator laid flat.

Many spiders, according to size

Cinnamon Dough Ornaments

Baking these in the oven does leave the house smelling great for the holiday season. They are also a lot of fun for kids to make and give as gifts.

1   **cup cinnamon**
½   **cup applesauce**

- Mix applesauce and cinnamon together in mixing bowl to form a stiff dough.
- Roll out dough to ¼ inch thickness.
- Press out shapes with cookie cutters and place on cooling rack to dry.
- Poke a hole in the top if making an ornament for the string. This should be done while the dough is still wet.
- These can air dry on cooling rack or they can be placed in the oven on the lowest setting to dry for 4 hours.

Popcorn Balls for Halloween

These wonderful treats can also be made for other holidays - just use appropriately colored gelatin.

1   **cup white sugar**
1   **cup corn syrup**
1   **(4 ounce) box gelatin - orange or berry black**
1   **cup popcorn, popped**

- In a small saucepan, combine sugar, syrup and gelatin. Bring to a rolling boil.
- Pour over popcorn. Stir to mix well; cool.
- When cool enough to handle, form into balls with well-buttered hands.

20 balls

Easy Reindeer Cookies

1   **(20 ounce) package refrigerated peanut butter cookie dough**
60 **(2 inch) pretzel twists**
60 **chocolate chips**
30 **red candy-coated chocolate pieces**

- Freeze dough for 15 minutes.
- Preheat oven to 350°.
- Slice dough into 30 (¼ inch) slices. Place 4 inches apart on ungreased cookie sheets. Using thumb and forefinger, pinch in each slice about ⅔ of the way down to shape face.
- Press a pretzel on each side of larger end for antlers. Press in chocolate chips for eyes.
- Bake for 9 to 11 minutes or until lightly browned.
- Remove from oven and press in red candy for the nose. Let stand 2 minutes; remove to wire racks to cool.

2½ dozen

Reindeer Chow

This is not only tasty for Santa's reindeer-it's great for people too!

1   **pound white chocolate, chopped**
3   **cups doughnut-shaped oat cereal**
3   **cups rice cereal squares**
3   **cups corn cereal squares**
2   **cups pretzel sticks**
2   **cups roasted peanuts**
1   **(12 ounce) bag candy-coated chocolate pieces**

- Slowly melt chocolate in microwave for 30 seconds at medium power. Stir and place back in microwave for another 30 seconds. Continue until all is melted and smooth. Do not overcook!
- Combine cereals, pretzels, peanuts and candy in large bowl.
- Spread mixture on a large cookie sheet and pour chocolate over all. Once cooled, break into pieces.

Peanut Butter and Jelly Popcorn

6   **cups popped popcorn**
2   **tablespoons butter**
2   **tablespoons peanut butter**
2   **tablespoons jelly**

- Place popcorn in a large bowl.
- In a small saucepan, over low heat, combine butter, peanut butter and jelly. Stir mixture constantly until jelly melts.
- Pour hot mixture over popcorn, tossing lightly to coat.

Serves 4 to 6

Popcorn Ball Trees

A fantasy forest for your gingerbread house.

1	cup popcorn kernels (DO NOT use microwave popcorn)
1	tablespoon salad oil
2	cups white sugar
1½	cups water
½	cup light corn syrup
1	teaspoon white vinegar
½	teaspoon salt
1	teaspoon vanilla
8-10	drops green food color

- Preheat oven to 300°.

- In a 4 quart pot, heat oil over high heat until a single kernel begins to bubble. Add remaining popcorn kernels, cover and shake pan to pop popcorn quickly.

- Remove unpopped kernels or burned popcorn. Place popcorn in a large oven-safe pan and place in oven.

- Grease the sides only of a 2 quart saucepan. Combine sugar, water, corn syrup, vinegar and salt. Over medium-high heat, cook to 250°, stirring frequently. Use a candy thermometer for this step. Watch closely!

- Remove from heat and stir in vanilla and food color. Remove popcorn from warm oven, and slowly pour candy mixture over popcorn. Stir gently until popcorn is coated evenly.

- Spray hands with vegetable cooking spray or rub with margarine. Using a sprayed measuring cup, scoop popcorn; with your hands shape into cones resembling evergreen trees - vary sizes. Place on greased cookie sheet to cool.

15 to 20 trees

Kids in the Kitchen

Before You Cook:

1. Always make sure your parents know that you're going to cook.

2. Always wash your hands with soap and warm water before handling food.

3. Read the recipe carefully before you begin.

4. Assemble all the ingredients and utensils listed in the recipe.

5. Clean up as you cook.

Edible Valentines

This is a fun way for children to make a Valentine present for their parents. If the child is old enough to read, they can spell out Valentines' messages with the cereal.

6	mini bagels or 3 English muffins
	Strawberry flavored cream cheese
	Alphabet-shaped cereal
	Marshmallows
	Colored sprinkles

- Split bagels or muffins in half; toast until lightly browned.
- Spread each half with cream cheese.
- Decorate as desired with cereal, marshmallows and sprinkles.

6 halves

P, B & J French Toast

8	white sandwich bread slices
4	teaspoons peanut butter
4	teaspoons jelly, any flavor desired
2	large eggs
¼	cup milk
1	tablespoon sugar
1	tablespoon butter
	Cinnamon

- Spread 4 slices of bread with teaspoon of peanut butter and 4 slices with 1 teaspoon of jelly. Place these two slices together and cut diagonally.
- In shallow bowl, combine eggs, milk, sugar and cinnamon; stir with a whisk
- Melt butter in a large nonstick skillet over medium heat. Dip the sandwiches into egg mixture, evenly coating both sides.
- Cook sandwich halves in batches, 2½ minutes on each side or until light brown.

Serves 4

Frozen Banana Pops

3   **large bananas**
6   **popsicle sticks**
1   **cup chocolate chips**
1   **tablespoon shortening**
½ **cup chopped nuts**

- Peel bananas and cut in half. Push a popsicle stick half way into each banana half.
- Wrap in foil and place in freezer overnight.
- Melt chocolate chips and shortening over low heat stirring constantly.
- Remove bananas from freezer and dip into melted chocolate then roll in chopped nuts.
- These can be re-wrapped and placed back in the freezer if not eaten right away.

Serves 6

Birthday Cones

2   **cups cold milk**
1   **(4 ounce) box instant pudding mix, any flavor**
6   **flat-bottomed ice cream cones**
    Prepared whipped cream
    Candy sprinkles

- Pour milk into small mixing bowl and add pudding mix. Beat with a wire whisk.
- Wait 5 minutes. Spoon pudding into ice cream cones.
- Freeze 3 hours. Top with whipped cream and sprinkles.

Serves 6

Butterfly Bites

3   stalks celery, washed
6   tablespoons spreadable Cheddar or cream cheese
12 twisted pretzels
    Raisins

- Cut celery in half crosswise. Fill each with 1 tablespoon cheese.
- Add a pretzel twist (wing) on each side. Add raisins for decorations on "back".

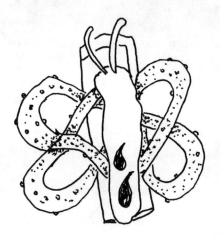

Mighty Milk

8   ice cubes
2   cups milk
2   bananas, peeled
4   tablespoons frozen orange juice concentrate

- In blender, combine ice cubes, bananas, and orange juice. Blend about 20 seconds. Pour into a frosty glass and enjoy.

Apple Smiles

2 **large apples**
½ **cup smooth peanut butter**
   Mini marshmallows

- Cut apples into eight slices each. Remove apple core.
- Spread peanut butter on one side of each slice.
- Place marshmallows on one slice and place slice on top.

This recipe should help your child through the loss of their first tooth. It recreates a toothless grin and helps the child see the humor in their "Apple Smile".

Serves 8

Mud

6 **whole graham crackers**
1 **(6 ounce) package instant chocolate pudding**
3 **cups cold milk**
   Paper cups
   Gummy worms
   Seeds (sunflower seeds, peanuts or candy-coated chocolate pieces)

- Place graham crackers in a large plastic bag with a zipper. Finely crush crackers.
- In a 1 quart jar, combine pudding and milk; shake for 2 minutes and pour into paper cups.
- Stir in cracker crumbs. Plant "seeds" and "worms".

Serves 6

People Bones

Make "dog bones" that people beg for.

½   **cup peanut butter**
½   **cup powdered milk**
1   **tablespoon honey**
2   **teaspoons graham cracker crumbs, finely crushed**

- In a small bowl, combine peanut butter, dry milk and honey. Mix very well.
- Divide dough into 6 pieces. Shape each piece to look like a dog bone.
- Sprinkle with cracker crumbs on both sides. Eat and enjoy!

Hot Cocoa Mix

Makes a wonderful Christmas gift for a teacher. Just store in a pretty Christmas tin; attach a gift card with instructions for serving.

1   **pound box hot cocoa mix**
1   **(8 quart) box instant nonfat dry milk**
1   **(6 ounce) jar non-dairy creamer**
1   **cup confectioners' sugar**
    Mini marshmallows

- In a very large bowl, combine cocoa mix, dry milk, creamer and sugar. Stir well.
- Store in an airtight container.
- For one serving add 6 tablespoons mix to 1 cup hot water. Stir well. Float marshmallows on top.

Edible Craft Dough Cookies

These cookies could be labeled "For Kids Only" - the dough looks and shapes remarkably like the colored craft dough that children often play with, the only difference is it's edible. Children can shape the dough the same way they do craft dough, or they can roll it and use cookie cutters.

1	cup butter or margarine, softened
1	cup shortening
2½	cups sifted confectioners' sugar
6	hard-boiled egg yolks, mashed
2	teaspoons baking soda
2	teaspoons cream of tartar
1	tablespoon vanilla extract
5	cups all-purpose flour
	Red, yellow and green food coloring paste

- Preheat oven to 350°.
- Cream butter and shortening; gradually add sugar, beating well at medium speed.
- Add egg yolks, baking soda, cream of tartar and vanilla, beating well.
- Gradually add flour, mixing well.
- Divide dough into 4 equal portions. Color one red, one yellow, one green and leave one plain. Wrap each separately in plastic wrap; chill at least 1 hour.
- Hand shape cookies into desired designs, or roll dough to ¼ inch thickness on a lightly floured surface and cut with 2½ inch cookie cutters. Place on ungreased cookie sheets.
- Bake for 8 to 10 minutes. Let cool on cookie sheets before removing to wire racks to finish cooling.

5½ dozen

Connie Maxwell Children's Home

In 1891, South Carolina Baptists secured a site for an orphanage in Greenwood, primarily through the loving generosity of Dr. J.C. and Sarah Maxwell. They had lost their 7 year old daughter, Connie to Scarlet Fever in 1883. The Maxwells donated more than 480 acres of land and their estate to be used in starting a ministry for children. The facility caters to children in grades K through 12, and assists its high school graduates with higher education needs. The children reside in 11 family-styled homes which are nestled in beautiful well-kept grounds.

Kids in the Kitchen

After You Cook:

1. Check to see that electric appliances are turned off and un-plugged.

2. Finish washing, rinsing and drying utensils.

3. Put all utensils and ingredients away.

4. Make sure the kitchen is neat and tidy.

Popcorn Cake

1   (16 ounce) bag miniature marshmallows
¾   cup vegetable oil
½   cup margarine or butter
5   quarts popped popcorn
1   (24 ounce) bag spiced gumdrops
1   cup salted peanuts

- In a large saucepan, melt marshmallows, oil and margarine until smooth.
- In a large bowl, combine popcorn, gumdrops and peanuts.
- Add marshmallow mixture and mix well.
- Press mixture into a well greased 10 inch tube pan (do not use 2 piece tube pan). Cover and refrigerate for at least 5 hours.
- Dip pan in hot water for 5 to 10 seconds to unmold. Slice cake with serrated or electric knife.

Serves 10 to 12

S'mores Indoors

These are great when you can't stand around a campfire to make this favorite treat.

1   (10 ounce) package marshmallows
    Wooden skewers
6   milk chocolate bars, melted
2   cups graham cracker crumbs

- Insert skewer in marshmallow. Dip in chocolate and roll in crumbs.

Many

Christmas
in the Kitchen

Special
Memorial
Tree

C. Marchi
© 2000

Christmas in the Kitchen

White Christmas

3 cups crisp rice cereal
1 cup flaked coconut
³⁄₄ cup powdered milk
¹⁄₂ cup confectioners' sugar
2 ounces candied fruit, chopped
2 ounces red and green candied cherries, chopped
¹⁄₄ cup raisins
4¹⁄₂ ounces white vegetable shortening, cut in small squares
4¹⁄₂ ounces white chocolate chips

- Brush a 9 x 13 inch dish with oil. Line base and sides with parchment paper.
- Combine cereal, coconut, milk, sugar, fruit, cherries and raisins in a large mixing bowl.
- In small saucepan, cook shortening and chocolate chips until melted and smooth.
- Combine chocolate mixture and cereal mixture. Press into prepared pan and refrigerate until set.
- Remove from pan, allow to stand 10 minutes. Cut into squares with sharp knife.

24 bars

"Mother would talk to me about how nice the chaplain was and how much she enjoyed his visits and prayers. Thank you. God Bless You."

Christmas Pizza

12 ounces semi-sweet chocolate chips
1 pound white almond bark, divided
2 cups mini marshmallows
1 cup crispy rice cereal
1 cup peanuts
16 ounces red maraschino cherries, quartered
3 tablespoons green cherries
⅓ cup coconut, flaked
1 teaspoon oil

- In a large saucepan, melt chocolate with 14 ounces of the almond bark over low heat, stirring until smooth. Remove from heat.
- Stir in marshmallows, cereal and peanuts. Pour into greased 12 inch pizza pan.
- Top with red and green cherries. Sprinkle with coconut.
- Melt remaining almond bark with oil over low heat; stirring until smooth. Drizzle over coconut. Chill.

Serves 10

Cranberry Decadent Cookies

8	ounces semi-sweet chocolate, chopped
¼	cup all-purpose flour
¼	cup cocoa powder
1	teaspoon cinnamon
⅛	teaspoon baking powder
	Pinch salt
6	tablespoons butter, softened
½	cup sugar
2	large eggs
1	cup white chocolate chips
1	cup dried cranberries

- Preheat oven to 350°.
- Grease large cookie sheets.
- Melt semi-sweet chocolate and cool.
- Combine flour, cocoa, cinnamon, baking powder and salt in bowl.
- In a large bowl, cream butter. Add sugar and beat until light and fluffy.
- Add eggs and beat until smooth. Stir in melted chocolate.
- Add dry ingredients and mix. Fold in white chocolate chips and cranberries.
- Drop by tablespoon on to cookie sheet.
- Bake 10 to 12 minutes, until cookies look dry and cracked but still feel soft when pressed lightly.
- Drizzle top of cookies with additional melted white chocolate chips.

2 dozen

Andrew Johnson Tailor Shop

Laurens County's most famous resident went on to become Governor of Tennessee, Vice-President of the United States under President Abraham Lincoln, and upon Lincoln's assassination, the 17th President of the United States. While in Laurens, President Johnson owned and operated a tailor shop on the town square.

"The home health aides were very wonderful caregivers and were always cheerful. My dad loved them and looked forward to seeing them."

Bourbon Pecan Cake

Marge Ball has been making this festive cake at Christmas for her family for 25 years.

2	**cups bourbon**
2	**cups red candied cherries**
2	**cups white seedless raisins**
2	**cups margarine or butter, softened**
2	**cups white sugar**
2	**cups dark brown sugar, firmly packed**
8	**eggs, separated**
5	**cups all-purpose flour, divided**
4	**cups pecan halves**
1½	**teaspoons baking powder**
1	**teaspoon salt**
2	**teaspoons nutmeg**

- Combine bourbon, cherries and raisins in large mixing bowl. Cover tightly and let stand in refrigerator overnight. Drain fruits and reserve bourbon.
- Preheat oven to 275°.
- Place butter in a large bowl of electric mixer and beat on medium speed until light and fluffy. Add sugars gradually, beating on medium speed until well blended.
- Add egg yolks, beating until well blended.
- Combine ½ cup flour with pecans.
- Sift remaining flour with baking powder, salt and nutmeg. Add 2 cups of flour mixture to the creamed mixture and mix thoroughly.
- Add reserved bourbon and remaining flour mixture alternately, ending with flour. Beat well after each addition.
- Beat egg whites until stiff, but not dry. Fold gently into cake batter.
- Add drained fruits and floured pecans to the cake batter; blend thoroughly.
- Grease a 10 inch tube pan; line bottom with waxed paper. Grease and lightly flour waxed paper. Pour cake batter into pan

Bourbon Pecan Cake *continued*

to within 1 inch of top. The remaining batter may be baked in a
small loaf pan, prepared the same way.

- Bake tube cake pan 4 hours and loaf cake pan 1½ hours, or
  until tester inserted comes out clean. Do not overbake.
- Cool cakes in pans on cake rack about 2 to 3 hours. Remove
  cakes from pans; remove wax paper.
- Wrap cakes in cheesecloth saturated with bourbon; then wrap
  in foil or plastic wrap and store in tightly covered container in
  refrigerator for several weeks.
- If desired, just before serving, beat together 1½ cups
  confectioners' sugar, 2 tablespoons hot milk and ¼ teaspoon
  vanilla extract. Spread over top of cake, allowing some to run
  down the sides.

Serves 25 to 30

White Russian Truffles

These make wonderful gifts at Christmas.

1¾ pounds milk chocolate, divided
1   cup whipping cream
¼   cup Kahlúa

- Chop finely 1 pound of the chocolate. Melt in a double boiler to 120°.

- Measure the cream into a 3 quart saucepan and bring just to the boil. Remove from the heat and cool to 120°. Add chocolate to the cooled cream and stir until the mixture is smooth.

- Stir the Kahlúa into the chocolate, mixing well. Scrape onto a baking sheet and refrigerate until chocolate is firm enough to form balls.

- Finely grate the remaining ¾ pound of chocolate. (This is easiest to do using the grater blade of a food processor.) Remove the filling from refrigeration and form into small rough balls. Place on a baking sheet lined with wax paper.

- Roll the truffles in the grated chocolate, pressing gently to adhere.

- Refrigerate overnight. Remove from refrigerator 15 minutes before serving.

Many

These truffles do not hold well at room temperature.

Orange Chocolate Truffles

⅓ **cup heavy cream**
¼ **cup butter**
6   **ounces semi-sweet chocolate chips**
2   **tablespoons orange zest**
1   **teaspoon orange extract**

• Stir the cream, butter and chocolate chips in a small heavy saucepan over medium heat until bubbling and chocolate is almost melted. Remove from heat. Stir until the chocolate is completely melted and mixture is smooth.

• Stir in the zest and extract.

• Pour the mixture into a shallow baking pan and refrigerate until firm enough to shape, about 40 minutes.

Coatings
   Ground pistachio nuts
   Unsweetened cocoa powder
   Confectioners' sugar
   Chocolate jimmies

• Spread 2 to 3 tablespoons of each coating ingredient in individual shallow dishes.

• Divide the cold chocolate mixture into 24 equal portions. Roll each portion into a ball. Roll the balls in the coating to cover completely. Place the balls as they are coated in 1 inch paper or foil bonbon cups.

• Store in an airtight container in the refrigerator for up to 2 weeks.

2 dozen

White Christmas Punch

"The home health aides were so gentle and mother really enjoyed her baths. We love all of you."

2   cups sugar
1   cup water
12 ounces evaporated milk
1½ teaspoons vanilla extract
1½ teaspoons almond extract
3   (½ gallon) cartons vanilla ice cream
6   (2 liter) bottles lemon-lime carbonated soda

- In a small saucepan, combine sugar and water. Stir constantly, cook over medium heat until sugar dissolves.
- Remove from heat; add evaporated milk, vanilla and almond extracts and let cool.
- Chill until ready to serve. Combine milk mixture, ice cream and soda in punch bowl just before serving. Stir thoroughly.

Serves 25 to 50

Holiday Brew

1   quart apple juice
1½ cups pineapple juice
2   tablespoons honey
2   tablespoons lemon juice
    Cinnamon sticks (4 inch)

- Combine apple juice, pineapple juice, honey, lemon juice and cinnamon sticks; bring to a boil.
- Remove from heat and discard cinnamon sticks. Serve hot.

1½ quarts

New Wave Eggnog

The cooked egg yolks make this the nog of choice for cooks who prefer to avoid raw eggs. Eggnog should be chilled at least 4 hours before serving and served within 24 hours.

4   **cups half-and-half**
1½ **cups sugar**
12 **large egg yolks**
½   **cup dark rum**
½   **cup brandy**
¼   **cup bourbon**
2   **cups heavy cream**
1   **pint high-quality vanilla ice cream**
     Freshly grated nutmeg, for serving

- In a medium saucepan over medium heat, stir the half-and-half with the sugar until the sugar dissolves and mixture is hot.

- In a medium bowl, whisk the egg yolks. Gradually whisk in some of the hot mixture. Return to the saucepan and cook over low heat, stirring constantly, until the mixture is thick enough to coat a spoon (a thermometer will read 180°), about 3 minutes.

- Strain into another medium bowl. Cool completely.

- Whisk in the rum, brandy and bourbon. Cover and refrigerate at least 4 hours.

- In a chilled, medium bowl, beat the heavy cream just until stiff. Fold into the chilled custard.

- Pour into a punch bowl and add the ice cream. Grate the nutmeg over the eggnog, and serve immediately.

Serves 16

Irish Cream

3   eggs
1¼ cups whiskey
1   (14 ounce) can sweetened condensed milk
1   teaspoon cream of coconut
1   teaspoon vanilla
3   tablespoons chocolate syrup

• Combine eggs, whiskey, milk, cream of coconut, vanilla and syrup in a blender for about 3 minutes.
• Keep refrigerated until ready to serve.

Serves 4 to 6

To complete the cookie jar mix, cut a 7 inch circle from festive cotton. Top jar lid with fabric circle; close with ring. Tie with ribbon and add gift tag with following instructions: Empty jar of cookie mix into mixing bowl; stir together. Add ½ cup butter or margarine, softened, 1 beaten egg and 1 teaspoon vanilla. Mix until completely blended. Roll into 1 inch balls; place 2 inches apart on ungreased cookie sheet. Bake at 375° about 12 to 14 minutes. Cool on wire racks.

Candy-Coated Chocolate Cookies in a Jar

2   cups all-purpose flour
½   teaspoon baking soda
½   teaspoon baking powder
1¼ cups sugar
1¼ cups candy-coated chocolate candies

• Mix together flour, soda and baking powder.
• In a wide-mouth 1 quart canning jar layer sugar, candies and flour mixture. Pack firmly.

2½ dozen

Use seasonally colored candies for different holidays.

Gingerbread Cookie Mix in a Jar

3½ cups all-purpose flour, divided
1   teaspoon baking powder
1   teaspoon baking soda
2   teaspoons ground ginger
1   teaspoon ground cloves
1   teaspoon cinnamon
1   teaspoon ground allspice
1   cup brown sugar, firmly packed

- Mix 2 cups of the flour with the baking powder and baking soda. Mix the remaining flour with the ginger, cloves, cinnamon and allspice.

- In a one quart, wide-mouth canning jar layer the flour/baking powder mixture, brown sugar and the flour/spice mixture.

- Attach gift tag to the jar with the following instructions: Empty contents of jar into a large mixing bowl. Blend together well.

- Add ½ cup butter softened, ¾ cup molasses and 1 slightly beaten egg. Mix until completely blended. Dough will be very stiff so you may need to use your hands. Cover and refrigerate for 1 hour.

- Preheat oven to 350°.

- Roll dough to ¼ inch thickness on a lightly floured surface. Cut into shapes with cookie cutter.

- Place cookies on a lightly greased cookie sheet about 2 inches apart.

- Bake for 10 to 12 minutes. Decorate.

18 cookies

Decorate jar lid with gingerbread fabric, fasten with rim. Attach gingerbread man cookie cutter with ribbon.

Chocolate Spoons

Chocolate coffee spoons are an elegant, flavorful melt away crowning touch to any cup of coffee. Decorate a pretty coffee mug, insert several spoons and a small package of coffee.

2	cups chocolate chips or white chocolate chips or candy melts
2	teaspoons solid shortening (optional)
35-45	heavy-duty plastic spoons
10-15	drops peppermint candy flavoring
3-4	candy canes, crushed
10-15	drops crème de menthe candy flavoring

- Cover cookie sheets with waxed paper.
- Place one cup of chocolate chips or candy melts in heat-proof measuring cup. (A smaller, deeper cup gives best results.) Microwave at 50% power for 1 minute. Remove cup and stir. Continue microwaving at 50% power, stirring every 30 seconds, until chocolate is melted and smooth. DO NOT overheat chocolate.
- To thin chocolate, add 1 teaspoon solid shortening per cup of chocolate. Stir gently. Dip plastic spoons in melted chocolate to cover the bowl of the spoon.
- Remove excess chocolate by tapping tip gently against the side of the measuring cup. Repeat with second cup of white chocolate.
- At this point, you may add candy flavorings, depending on which flavor you decide. Add 5 to 7 drops peppermint or crème de menthe flavoring to each cup of chocolate.
- For Candy Cane Spoons, press chocolate spoon into crushed candy, holding spoon at a diagonal. Place on cookie sheet and cool.
- Wrap spoons with plastic wrap and tie with a pretty ribbon.

35 to 45 spoons

Holiday Bath Salts

Candy Cane Bath Salts

12	**tall jelly (12 ounce) canning jars with lid and rings**
2	**(4 pound) cartons Epsom Salts**
4	**pounds sea salt or Kosher salt**
½	**teaspoon glycerin, divided**
12-15	**drops peppermint oil**
12-15	**drops red food coloring**

- Empty 1 carton Epsom Salts into large mixing bowl. Add 3 cups sea salt or Kosher salt. Mix well. Add ¼ teaspoon glycerin and 6 to 8 drops oil. Mix well.

- In second large mixing bowl, empty one carton Epsom Salts, and add 3 cups sea salt. Stir well. Add ¼ teaspoon glycerin, 6 to 8 drops oil and food color. Stir until completely blended. Color should be even.

- Holding jars at an angle, layer salts in jars, alternating white and colored mixes.

- Use decorative lids on jars. Add rings; gift tags tied with ribbon may be added.

12 jars

For Peaches 'n Cream Bath Salts use 12 to 15 drops peach essential oil and 12 to 15 drops orange food color.

"We deeply appreciate your care. Without you, our situation would have been very difficult. Thank you."

Gourmet Cookie Mix in a Jar

1   cup all-purpose flour
½   teaspoon baking powder
½   teaspoon baking soda
1¼ cups rolled oats
1   (5.5 ounce) milk chocolate bar
½   cup white sugar
½   cup brown sugar, firmly packed
½   cup chopped pecans
½   cup chocolate chips
1   wide mouth canning jar with lid and ring
1   (9 inch) circle appropriate fabric

- With wire whisk, mix flour, baking powder and baking soda. Pour into jar and pack down level with heavy object.
- Mix oatmeal in food processor. Grate chocolate bar and mix into the oatmeal. Pack on top of flour in jar.
- Add white sugar and pack tightly. Add brown sugar and pack tightly.
- Layer nuts on top of sugar; layer chocolate chips over nuts until even with top.
- Cover lid with fabric and secure with rubber band at neck of jar. Tie with ribbon to cover rubber band. Add gift card with the following directions:
- Gourmet Cookies - Preheat oven to 375°. Spoon chocolate chips and nuts into small bowl, set aside. Spoon brown and white sugar into mixing bowl, add ½ cup butter or margarine, cream until light and fluffy. Add 1 egg and ½ teaspoon vanilla; mix well. Pour oatmeal and flour mixture from jar into bowl; mix thoroughly. Roll into 1 inch balls, place on slightly greased cookie sheet 2 inches apart. Bake for 8 to 10 minutes.

3 dozen

This mix keeps for 10 to 12 weeks after mixing.

Gifts from the Kitchen

Beautiful Brownies

12	wide mouth quart-size canning jars with lids and rings
8	teaspoons salt
13½	cups all-purpose flour, divided
4	cups cocoa
8	cups brown sugar
8	cups white sugar
3	(12 ounce) bags chocolate chips
3	(12 ounce) bags white chocolate chips
6	cups chopped pecans
12	(7 inch) circles of holiday fabric
	Ribbon

- In each jar, layer ingredients as follows: ⅔ teaspoon salt, ⅝ cup flour, ⅓ cup cocoa, ½ cup flour, ⅔ cup brown sugar, ⅔ cup white sugar, ½ cup chocolate chips, ½ cup white chocolate chips and ½ cup pecans.

- Close jar with lid and ring. Top each jar with fabric and tie with ribbon.

- Instruction card included with gift tag should read: Preheat oven to 350°. Grease 1 (9 x 9 inch) baking dish. Pour the contents of the jar into a large bowl and mix well. Stir in 1 teaspoon vanilla, ⅔ cup vegetable oil and 3 eggs. Beat just until mixed. Pour batter into pan and bake for 20 to 25 minutes.

Bird Seed Wreath

1   package frozen bread dough
1   egg yolk, beaten
**   Bird seed**

- Preheat oven to 350°.
- Make a wreath out of workable dough, brush with egg yolk and dash of water for glaze.
- Press in lots of bird seed before baking. Bake for 30 minutes.
- When cool, tie with ribbon and bow for hanging.

When making this wreath for a gift, attach this note to it:

"So you think
I'm a stollen?

You could be
quite right.

But, please,
do be careful and
don't take a bite!

I'm really a wreath
for inside decor

To be hung on a wall,
or even a door.

Then…

About the same
time you take down
your tree,

Place me outside
and you will see,

I'm for the birds!
(The bread and the seed)

Wind the
holidays up with your
special deed!"

HospiceCare of the Piedmont, Inc. wishes to thank the volunteers, Bereaved families, Board members and staff for sharing their treasured recipes. Without the support of these people, it would not be possible to have developed this cookbook. We regret that we were unable to include all recipes submitted due to similarity or availability of space. We are truly grateful to everyone who contributed so generously to *Cooking With Care*.

Robbie Able
Nina Adams
Ruby Adams
Gwen Amann
Millie Amrick
Debra Bagwell
Marge Ball
Angie Barnhart
Cheryl Barnhart
Laura Barnhart
Cathy Bauer
Pam Bazzle
Linda Bell
Henry Black
Hal Black
Maudie Black
Patsy Black
Nancy Boyle
Barbara Brookshire
Helen Brown
Kanda Brunson
Kelly Buckshorn
Jan Burton
Ginny Butler
Dena Byrd
Virginia Cambreling
Karen Carr
Joan Carter
Virginia Caughman
Tracey Caughman
Peggy Cheezem
Emma Clary
Ruby Clark
Sudie Moore Clem

Catherine Coates
Jenny Cobb
Chris Cooley
Linda Cooley
Nancy Corley
Jean Crawford
Betty Curry
Goldie Davis
Jenny Dunlap
Kathy Ecklund
Etolia Elledge
Betty Ann Ellenberg
Mary Ellis
Lynn Elliott
Toni Ferqueron
Larry Frakes
Tillie Freeland
Hannah B. Gantt
Fran Garland
Wilma Giles
Sheila Gilmer
Ruth Goldman
Deborah Gray
Mary Ellen Guido
Perrin Hall
Mary Hamrick
Marlene Hatcher
Bettie Horne
Delsie Horne
Nina Horne
Sabra Horne
Pat Horton
Garnet Johnson
Vivian Kelley

Nancy Kier
Estelle Kirby
Pam Latham
Jewel Lee
Margery Lightsey
Bill Logan
Mary Lusk
Hazel Manos
Cam Marchi
Teresa Marchi
W. Regan Marshall
Colleen Martin
Gwen Martin
Modjeska Martin
Liz Masters
Linda Miller
Sandy Moffett
Leslie Monroe
Cindy Morris
Judy Morton
Dee Mountford
Marcella Mundy
Marilyn Murphy
Mary McAllister
Margie McBurnett
Irene McClain
Kym Newton
Catherine Nicholson
Patty Nicholson
Tricia Nicholson
Mary Olsen
Tomoko Ono
Barbara Parham
Eloise Parker

Lunette Patten
Vera Reynolds
Vickie Riedel
Sharon Rinehart
Jane Roper
Diane Rushton
Bonnie Sawyer
Sallie Schisler
Dane Sergeant
Margie Shew
Cathy Elaine Smith
Elsie Horne Smith
Jackie Smith
Nell Perry Squires
Pat Stargel
Betty Stockman
Carolyn Strom
Nancy Suttlemyre
Tom Suttlemyre
Michelle Terry
Peggy Ticehurst
Beth Treaster
Sonny Tuck
Sandy Walter
Melissa Shew Warner
Gayle Werts
Louise Willoughby
Carolyn Willy
Cathy Wilusz
Rosemary Winkler
David Yingling
Catherine Young
Susanne Young

Index

Cooking With Care 🕊 245

Index

C

CABBAGE

CARROTS

CASSEROLES

CEREALS AND GRAINS *(also see Rice)*

CHEESE

D

DESSERTS

Index

Index

Cooking With Care 🕊 **251**

Index

R

S

SALAD DRESSINGS

SALADS

SEAFOOD

SOUPS

Index

HospiceCare of the Piedmont, Inc. Cookbook

408 West Alexander Avenue
Greenwood, South Carolina 29646
(864)227-9393 Office (864)227-9377 Fax

Please send me _____ copies of *Cooking With Care*   @ $19.95 each _____

South Carolina residents add sales tax   @   1.20 each _____

Postage and handling   @   5.00 each _____

Total Enclosed _____

Please mail above cookbook(s) to:

Name _____

Address _____ Telephone (   ) _____

City _____ State _____ Zip _____

Make checks payable to HospiceCare.
Please do not send cash. Sorry no C.O.D.'s
Mail to above address.

HospiceCare of the Piedmont, Inc. Cookbook

408 West Alexander Avenue
Greenwood, South Carolina 29646
(864)227-9393 Office (864)227-9377 Fax

Please send me _____ copies of *Cooking With Care*   @ $19.95 each _____

South Carolina residents add sales tax   @   1.20 each _____

Postage and handling   @   5.00 each _____

Total Enclosed _____

Please mail above cookbook(s) to:

Name _____

Address _____ Telephone (   ) _____

City _____ State _____ Zip _____

Make checks payable to HospiceCare.
Please do not send cash. Sorry no C.O.D.'s
Mail to above address.